PROBLEMS OF WAR AND PEACE
IN THE SOCIETY OF NATIONS

PROBLEMS OF WAR
AND PEACE
IN THE SOCIETY OF
NATIONS

LECTURES ARRANGED BY THE
UNIVERSITY OF CALIFORNIA COMMITTEE
ON INTERNATIONAL RELATIONS

SECOND SERIES
DELIVERED AUTUMN 1937

Essay Index Reprint Series

BOOKS FOR LIBRARIES PRESS
FREEPORT, NEW YORK

First Published 1937
Reprinted 1967

INTERNATIONAL STANDARD BOOK NUMBER:
0-8369-0270-X

LIBRARY OF CONGRESS CATALOG CARD NUMBER:
67-23188

PRINTED IN THE UNITED STATES OF AMERICA

CONTENTS

PREFACE

IN THE FALL OF 1936 a series of seven lectures entitled "The United States Among the Nations"* was arranged by the University of California Committee on International Relations. The lectures were intended, in their entirety, to present a picture of American foreign policy in the light of our historic past and of the present world situation. The addresses were well received, and it was decided not only to publish them, thus making them available to a wider audience, but also to present annually a similar series of lectures, each of which should deal with one of the vital contemporary issues in the field of international relations.

The theme for the series of 1937 was: "Problems of War and Peace in the Society of Nations." The causes of war, and the most effective means of attaining peace and security in these insecure times, have become a subject of debate throughout the world. Fascists, socialists, and defenders of the democratic tradition offer different diagnoses of the fundamental malady from which international society suffers and of the remedy that is indicated. It is hoped that the present series of lectures will contribute to a better understanding, by the student body and the general public, of these varying viewpoints, and to a more accurate assessment of their value in pointing the way toward a better world order.

The six addresses contained in this volume were delivered in Berkeley on successive Wednesday evenings from Septem-

---

* Published by the University of California Press, Berkeley, California, 1937.

ber 22 to October 27, 1937, by members of the faculty of the University of California. They are here presented in approximately the form in which they were delivered.

THE GREAT COMMUNITY

———

EDWIN D. DICKINSON
EMANUEL S. HELLER PROFESSOR OF LAW
DEAN OF THE SCHOOL OF JURISPRUDENCE
IN THE UNIVERSITY OF CALIFORNIA

Lecture delivered September 22, 1937

THE GREAT COMMUNITY

SOMEWHERE in prehistoric space and time, groups of primitive people became vaguely conscious of their intergroup relationships. This was the genesis of that extraordinary phenomenon which today we call the community of nations. It was probably somewhat later in the evolution of intergroup relationships that primitive people became conscious of the habits or customs which were tending to shape their conduct, in relation to the members of other groups, in conformity with primitive patterns. This was the genesis of the jurisprudence of nations which more recently we have come to call international law. We may surmise that these emerging concepts were long concerned chiefly with the carrying on or with the conclusion of hostilities. The cultivation of primitive commerce probably came later and less heroic patterns must have developed with glacial slowness. In any case, associations more cosmopolitan than those of tribe or totem or family had emerged out of creation's welter. We need not pause to inquire what savage covetousness or fear may have first produced such associations. From the moment of their first faint impact upon the primitive mind, there was in progress the development of a greater community of peoples.

This development appears to have progressed through two grand cycles and to be at present substantially advanced upon a third. The first was the age of discovery. This was also the prehistoric age and its interpretation belongs to the anthropologist rather than the historian. Men discovered other groups than those with which they were immediately associated.

[3]

They became conscious of more or less important relationships between their own groups and others. They became aware of the patterns with which the conduct of such relationships was tending more and more to conform. The earliest patterns were probably concerned, as suggested, with self-help and with the crudest of limitations upon physical violence. The foreigner was always a potential if not an actual enemy. Nonhostile intercourse was but a feeble prediction of later developments. The sanctions which compelled a measure of respect for primitive customs were characteristically the taboo or superstition and primitive priesthoods served as the oracles of a slowly expanding practice.

The next grand cycle was the age of integration. This age is faintly forecast in the earliest of historic records. Self-help continued the dominating interest; but nonhostile intercourse was growing slowly in relative importance. The intercourse of groups was divided into war and peace, with some attention to hostile measures short of war, and with increasingly elaborate rituals for determining the transition from one condition to the other. With the accumulation of records and the progress of learning, there was conscious effort not only to record and interpret custom, but eventually to understand the rights and duties of nations as an integrated system. The substance of it all was practice in conformity with nature, a nature which smiled tolerantly upon peace while also giving its blessing to the just war. The sanctions were religion and morality; oracles were found ultimately in the great theologians, philosophers, and jurists; and in their writings the age flowered valiantly at the very time that colonial expansion and a nascent industrialism were preparing new strains and tests for the frail structure of international society.

✓ The third grand cycle, initiated chiefly by forces released in the Industrial Revolution, and now in its second century of misadventure, will probably be known as the age of construction. Is this an overbold attempt to interpret what is essentially our own time? Is it indeed presumptuous to suggest even a clue to the significance of an age that is still so young? Although we are necessarily denied perspective with respect to our own time, and perforce bewildered by many voices which will ultimately be completely forgotten, there are persuasive reasons for believing that the time when our own America became one of the community of nations was very close to one of the grand transitions of international progress, and, further, that this transition was to be marked by a new emphasis upon creative statesmanship in international relations.

At the end of the eighteenth century the physical world was at least superficially known. Devices for the dissemination of learning had been brought to an unprecedented perfection. The church had ceased definitely to serve as a single unifying factor. Our own revolution had lighted a small but luminous torch in North America and the French Revolution was scattering its fires among the combustible rubbish heaps of Europe. An economic revolution of unprecedented scope and violence was beginning to change profoundly the manner of living of large masses of the world's population, to stimulate the tremendous forces of population growth, and to focus attention as never before upon the exploitation of the

world's physical resources. Central and South America were
approaching political separation from Europe. The opening
of Africa and Asia to Western influences was not far in the
future. In brief, there was emerging a new community of
peoples, having its roots in an earlier age, rapidly becoming
global in contrast with earlier continental communities, and
pulsing in the intimacies of an interdependence which followed swiftly upon invention and industrialization.

As tendencies of the nineteenth century were revealed, it
became evident that the community of nations was being
remolded by the dynamic forces of a new age. The idea of
community had come to epitomize at least the more elemental and obvious facts of international life. As integrated and
rationalized after the revival of learning, the community of
nations stood forth as an institutional development made inevitable by the growth of populations and their competitive
exploitation of the world's resources. In our own country,
when Chief Justice Jay charged the first federal grand juries
in 1790, he began by stressing the obvious and fundamental
proposition that we had "become a nation" and as such were
"responsible to others for the observance of the law of nations." With the swift improvement of transportation and
communication and the rapid growth of machine industry,
accompanied by new divisions of labor among the peoples
of the world, it was impressed more and more deeply upon
the consciousness of thoughtful men everywhere that neither
revelation nor the mere rationalization of accumulated experience could assure security. There were new and imperative
demands for creative statesmanship. Much as the engineer's

handiwork was contributing to the conquest and control of physical forces, the conscious planning of new principles and institutions had become essential to the mastery of intangible nature. For sanctions the world must depend more and more upon an intelligent and farsighted understanding of mutual interest. As integration yielded to construction, the great jurist was to become less of an oracle and more of an amanuensis to statesmen.

In retrospect we are able to discern the prelude of a great creative effort in the growing volume of national legislation concerned with international affairs. It was becoming the fashion to supplement or even supplant the revealed or judge-discovered law by the made-law of legislatures; and this process was soon invoked to supplement such fragments of the national law as concerned the rights and duties of nations. In setting a new style in constitution making in 1787, the people of the United States expressly delegated to their national legislature the power "to define and punish piracies and felonies committed on the high seas and offenses against the law of nations." In 1794, the United States established a notable precedent in the enactment of its first neutrality legislation. Laws for the suppression of all manner of piracies on the sea were enacted in important maritime countries and the long struggle to outlaw the detestable slave trade by statute was begun. The counterfeiting of foreign moneys was denounced as vigorously as offenses against the national currency. Laws for the protection of the official representatives of other states were enacted and amplified. Legislation conceived to foster and govern a swiftly growing international commerce appeared upon the statute books; and laws for giving effect to the obligations of treaties were added to the mounting volume of national legislation dealing constructively with matters of international concern.

The first notes of the prelude were hardly recorded when it became evident that national law making was quite incapable of responding adequately to the insistent needs of a society of growing interdependence. Convinced by swiftly changing conditions that national efforts must be supplemented, the nations found in treaties a means of more effective coöperation. Before the nineteenth century, for example, common crime had hardly become a matter of international concern. The criminal who committed an offense in Paris was ordinarily apprehended in Paris and punished by the Paris authorities. In any case, he rarely escaped from France. With increasing facility of communication and travel in the nineteenth century, it became easier to escape from France than it was in the eighteenth century to escape from Paris; and it also became proportionately easier to complicate the difficulties of national authorities by committing crimes across international frontiers. The best-planned national legislation was relatively ineffective and early in the nineteenth century the nations began to extend the practice of making treaties for the mutual return of fugitives from justice. Presently the world was well-nigh covered with an intricate network of carefully formulated extradition treaties. Less dramatic, but even more significant, was the rapid multiplication of treaties which opened great rivers to navigation and seaports to shipping under other flags, removed barriers to trade and travel, assured a minimum of privilege to merchants and others of alien race, and facilitated the development of the modern consular system. In literally thousands of treaties the nations were seeking to build a polity responsive to the needs of a changing social order.

The achievements of treaty making soon suggested an even more ambitious use of the treaty process. An increasingly complex and fluid international life required new law, new procedures, and new institutions, no less than coöperation amplified through the multiplication of bilateral agreements, a new strategy of progress no less than revised tactics in the employment of improved devices. Cautiously at first, eventually on a much more ambitious scale, the treaty process was generalized and made the instrument of international legislation. In the long struggle to outlaw the slave trade, for example, national legislation inaugurated the movement. Bilateral agreements among nations supplemented national legislation, but could hardly bring the movement to fruition. A famous clause inserted in the Treaty of Vienna in 1815 recognized the necessity for collective action. Near the end of the century, collective action was achieved in the General Act of Brussels of 1890; and the Slavery Convention of 1926 incorporates the latest of international legislation for the suppression of slavery and the international slave trade.

More recently the same process has been invoked to denounce and stamp out the white-slave traffic. It is perhaps more than a suggestion of the respect in which the process is held that on one occasion the traders in prostitutes called their own secret international congress to combat measures of suppression. Certainly no more contemptible body of rogues ever gathered together. There were eighty-nine representatives of the nefarious traffic in attendance from different countries; and it is some satisfaction to know that the police learned of their gathering, surrounded in Warsaw their place of meeting, and arrested the entire congress. Slowly but relentlessly the same process of law making has been pressing back toward ultimate control the traffic in drugs and narcotics. There is a warning for those who have been engaged in exploiting the international trade in munitions. Recent investigations have revealed something of the extent to which this traffic has become a menace to orderly international life. Processes tried and tested are at hand; and it is hardly to be doubted that they will be used with increasing effect as the facts with respect to the traffic are disclosed.

Constructive international legislation has been used with even more significant effect, though in circumstances less dramatic, to build a régime of international intercourse which is in some measure responsive to modern conditions of industry and commerce. There is no time to dwell with the emphasis which it deserves upon this important aspect of a significant movement. We may only take note that the process has been invoked to unify in international trade our systems of weights and measures, to organize and perfect the international régime of postal, telegraphic, and radio communication, to promote common interests in travel and commerce, whether by land, by sea, or by air, to unify the principles of our commercial law, to suppress counterfeiting, to secure through general copyright, patent, and trade-mark treaties the mutual protection of essential interests in literary, artistic, or industrial property, to fortify an interdependent community of peoples against the spread of plague or pestilence, to modernize and improve the whole system of international transit and communication, and to establish basic conditions of industrial labor of sufficient integrity to resist the vicious downward spiral of unregulated international competition.

Perhaps the importance of the general movement is revealed most clearly to those who are familiar with the scope of contemporary effort to internationalize modern labor legislation. The conditions which were produced by the rise of the modern factory system have respected no national frontiers. The alleviation in one country of the occupational diseases or of the physical and moral degeneration produced by long hours, low wages, child labor, and unhealthy working conditions has frequently had as its chief effect the migration of industry to another country where humanity and foresight were less mature. Thus there has emerged from the complications of modern industrial life a new cosmopolitan legislation. An effort to serve this interest was initiated before the Great War by voluntary and unofficial organizations. Treaties prohibiting night work for women in industry and forbidding the use of the deadly white phosphorous in match manufacture were approved by a number of states. After the war, this movement, sponsored by an International Labor Organization in which employers, governments, and labor were each to have an effective voice, spread with extraordinary rapidity. At the present moment, owing to the initiative of this Organization and of the vast interests which it represents, the world is being covered by a system of labor treaties dealing with the principal aspects of the modern labor problem. Much swifter and more effective than the spread of bilateral treaties of extradition in the nineteenth century, the movement is encompassing the earth with at least the rudiments of a modern labor code. To all who would understand the significant tendencies of the time, a study of this important aspect of our recent progress may be emphatically commended.

Without dwelling longer upon the movement, we may assert with no fear of contradiction that the record of one hundred years of international legislation affords significant evidence of the capacity of nations to deal constructively with the economic and social forces which have been released in a new age. Of comparable significance has been the planning and creating of more effective procedure; for international life is an evolution, the laws of this life are a process, and successful adjustment depends as much upon the procedures available as upon the principles of conduct which may be accepted at any given time. Here, again, whatever the harvest of a season, the tendencies have been profoundly encouraging.

Consider in passing the improvements made in the organization and conduct of ordinary intercourse among members of the great community. Impressive strides have been taken since the day when pompous emissaries, accompanied by their retinues of courtiers and henchmen, went to "lie abroad" at the courts of suspicious sovereigns. The modern diplomatic and consular staff has become a complicated organization of experts in many fields; the service in most countries is a profession of secure tenure; and the trained personnel that is now sent to "lie abroad" has been made a vastly more efficient and sensitive instrument of orderly intercourse. Notwithstanding the niggardly sums which are usually appropriated for its support, in comparison with the sums available for the armed force, the foreign office in the modern government renders effective service in a world in which every new invention seems to increase the hazards of normal international life. What we might accomplish in real preparedness for peace, by providing an adequate support for a trained, imaginative, and responsible foreign service in every great country, is surely one of the challenging questions of our time.

Consider the strides that have been taken in the development and improvement of the procedures for more formal adjustment through arbitration, adjudication, or conciliation. The narrative is now many times a twice-told tale. It is unnecessary to review the development of improved procedures in the last century, to call attention to the network of treaties in which such procedures are made more easily available, or to emphasize anew the results which have been achieved through these procedures in liquidating war claims, settling boundary disputes, disposing of an infinite variety of claims founded upon an asserted injury to the person or property of nationals, resolving difficult questions with respect to the exploitation of the resources of the sea, deciding questions of territorial sovereignty, adjusting conflicts of jurisdiction, or settling disputes with respect to the interpretation of treaties. It is much more important that something should be said of the significance of this progress, that emphasis should be placed upon the trends disclosed; for we may hardly fail to discern the evidences of a new expression of creative effort which seeks to build procedures of adjustment adequate for contemporary international life. In our crowded urban communities, where millions of human beings jostle one another in hurried pursuit of the pleasures and necessities of living, we have been compelled to construct new methods of social adjustment in order to make life possible. In the society of nations, in like manner, the relentless march of science and invention is making of the human species a crowded community in which nations inevitably jostle one another. New procedures of adjustment have become equally imperative and the capacity to create them has been demonstrated.

Consider the extraordinary development which has taken place in recent years in the procedure of international conference. Groups of people living in proximity to one another, no less than individuals in neighborhood, are certain to have their conflicts and their common interests. In the adjustment of one or the promotion of the other, conference is the beginning of collective wisdom. It is only through conference that there can come mutual understanding, the discovery of means of adjustment, or the planning of useful coöperation. As the great age of integration was approaching its climax, the modern procedure of conference was inaugurated with a vast display of pomp and ceremony. It was first invoked only on great occasions to liquidate war or prepare for an interval of precarious peace. Its preparations were cumbersome, costly, and protracted. In at least one famous instance, the procedure moved so slowly that armies were reassembled and on the march before the men of state could come to grips with the serious business of the day. Even in the nineteenth century, when conferences were called at more frequent intervals to plan for constructive coöperation, it was necessary to re-create almost every detail of organization and procedure for each new conference. Governments vied with one another for the honor of extending the invitation. Days might drag into months or months into years before the list could be agreed upon and the preparatory work completed. Indeed, it was not until the organization of permanent offices at Geneva, to serve the League of Nations after the Great War, that the procedure of international conference as we now know it came into common use. Through the offices at Geneva and by means of a technique which has become familiar, the preparations for each new meeting are made efficiently and swiftly by the same expert staff which has planned for previous conferences. The procedure has made possible a most impressive series of useful meetings dealing with almost every subject of conceivable international interest. This has been, without question, one of the League's most useful achievements. Its record indicates that there is latent among members of the great community not only a capacity for construction, but also a capacity which may be utilized swiftly and effectively whenever there is a real will to achieve.

Since it is ultimately through some form of administration that law and procedure are translated into effective action, a community of nations conscious of its capacity to create new law and new procedures was certain to envisage sooner or later a need for new institutions of government. The challenge of new economic and social conditions soon set astir in the nineteenth century new developments within the governments of industrial countries. Not only was the foreign office, the traditional agency of intercourse with other nations, required to expand its activities, create new services, and undertake tasks which were unknown in the eighteenth century, but also every major department of national administration became responsible for affairs of international importance. Departments charged with the administration of finance, communication, commerce, or labor became at times almost as conscious of the international ramifications of their problems as ministries of foreign affairs or defense. Some of their problems, indeed, admitted as little of an effective national administration, without substantial international coöperation, as problems of peace or war. As the century advanced, international institutions were established at Berne, Brussels, Paris, and elsewhere, to supplement and fortify the efforts of national administration. Communication, navigation, health, commerce, and labor provided the subject-matter of a new coöperative undertaking. Although voluntary and of closely guarded authority, these new institutions were indicative of a growing consciousness of at least some of the more obvious consequences of international interdependence. After the Great War, international administration was substantially reorganized and amplified at Geneva. It is in this field, in which the Covenant rested securely upon a substantial experience, that the League of Nations has done some of its most useful and enduring work.

A community in which constructive effort was beginning to produce new law, new procedures, and new institutions of administration could hardly fail to envisage as an essential aspect of its progress the creation of institutions for the judicial settlement of international disputes. The growing volume of national court decisions affecting matters of international interest was at least suggestive. The success of national courts under a federal system of government bestirred the imagination to conceive of courts constituted for a larger community. Successful arbitration in historic controversies resolved at Geneva, Washington, and elsewhere, encouraged confidence that a dream might be translated into reality. Increasing resort to specially created tribunals to dispose of accumulated claims advanced by one nation in behalf of its nationals against another served to amplify experience. The Permanent Court of International Arbitration at The Hague was inaugurated at the end of the nineteenth century and tested in the early years of the twentieth century. After the Great War, a long and patient effort to create an agency of justice among nations which might be really permanent and truly judicial was brought at last to fruition in the Permanent Court of International Justice. While no mere judicial body, national or international, can give the ultimate answer to a question of peace or war, these achievements of a few brief generations are significant evidence of the tendencies of creative effort in this latest age. Those who are skeptical of the movement or who belittle its importance in our present community life should cultivate historical perspective as well as familiarity with the institutions which are already at our service.

It is no exaggeration to say that the creation of new law within and between nations has secured a minimum of order where less than order must have led inevitably to friction and futile strife, that new procedures have given confidence in order where want of confidence must have promoted disintegration and anarchy, that the building of new institutions of administration and justice has kept nations in some measure abreast of their growing interdependence and has illuminated the avenues of an effective progress. It is not undue pessimism, on the other hand, to concede that the contacts and conflicts of modern international life have multiplied rapidly, at times more rapidly than the nations have been able to build. Consultation and conference have come to be regarded as the ultimate recourse when difficulties multiply or disaster threatens. Conference, indeed, has become more than an international procedure. It has emerged as an essential institution of orderly community life. The Pan American Conferences, the so-called Peace Conferences at The Hague, and the innumerable conferences of the League of Nations at Geneva are only the latest phase of a movement which has been gathering momentum for at least three generations. Every plan for implementing old covenants or preparing new ones calls for more effective organization of the meetings of nations. We are challenged to appraise the achievements of this movement, and to take stock of its failures, as we continue to build for an international life of order and security. No one can view the contemporary international scene with satisfaction. Yet only the uninformed visionary would ignore accumulated experience, disregard fundamental tendencies, or build castles in Spain when more substantial materials are at our disposal.

As the superficial order and security of the Victorian interval recede in somewhat romantic memories, the world immediately about us seems baffling in its complexity and fluidity. Approximately two billion human beings are struggling to conserve and improve life on this planet. They are organized locally in more than threescore states or amorphous political bodies, among which there is at once an approach to type and an extraordinary diversity of characteristics and interests resulting from differences in race, culture, religion, geography, economic resource, historic antecedents, and other basic factors. There are organized populations which are reckoned in many millions and others which could be accommodated in a single suburb of one of the world's great cities. There are populations which find strength in numbers and others in which numerical greatness is a source of real weakness. There are empires upon whose territory the sun sets but briefly and diminutive political bodies whose entire domain could be encompassed by an aerial camera. There are countries dominated by a single race and others distracted by the rivalries of race within their borders. There are peoples who are fortunate in geographic location and economic resource and other less fortunate peoples who must perforce extract their livelihood with difficulty from an increasingly reluctant soil. World maps are a labyrinthian patchwork of languages, religions, and cultures. The problems of order and security among the members of such a community are bound to be difficult enough.

In our own time there have been added to the ordinary difficulties of international life the problems of readjustment

which were left as a heritage from the Great War. Generations yet unborn will be compelled to share the material and
spiritual cost of that disastrous adventure. The opportunity
which came after the war to bind up wounds and prepare
for real reconciliation was permitted to pass. While statesmen
were struggling to control the disintegrating forces of political nationalism, the rising tides of economic nationalism
frustrated their efforts. More recently, among defeated and
disillusioned peoples, racial nationalism has raised its ugly
head. Fascism seeks countenance by opposing socialism, and
both are contemptuous of democracy. Humiliated at Adowa
and Caporetto, and struggling to support a growing population upon an old and tired soil, Italy has revolted against the
existing international order. Made conscious of strength at
Mukden and Port Arthur, disappointed at Paris and Washington, its trade harassed by disturbance in China and its
future rendered precarious by a mounting birth rate, Japan
has ignored its covenants and swept over the Asiatic main-
land. Crushed and humiliated in a disastrous war, stripped
of sea power and colonies, hemmed in by alliances, and frustrated by want of raw materials for its industries or markets
for its products, Germany awaits only a favorable opportunity
to throw down the gage of battle. A great fear has spread
over the world, generating violence of thought, word, and
action. All this, notwithstanding the bitter lessons of four
tragic years still within the memory of a large proportion of
the world's people.

Less than twenty years ago we knew that war, once regarded as the colorful and legitimate recourse of an aggrieved

nation, had become the most terrible of all revolutions. We knew that wars involving the great industrial nations could no longer be localized and permitted to spend their disastrous effect without involving others. With an approach to equilibrium between the contesting forces, we knew that no nation could really win a great war by mere military victory. We knew that even the threat of war between great nations tended at once to draw others into the opposing scales to produce an equilibrium. We knew that wealth had become so intangible, the economic structure so closely knit, that the more ruthless the war the more surely both victors and vanquished were defeated. We knew, or at least we should have known, that "a war to end war" was the most bizarre and futile catchword that ever piped a hysterical people off to destruction.

Are these and other tragic lessons so soon forgotten? The madness of destruction had its momentary triumph after 1914. Must we destroy again on a still more colossal scale before we resume construction? This is at once the supreme question of the day and a question no one can answer. We can only say that the incredible folly of it should restrain even those who have lost all sense of moral values. Watt and Nobel and Edison and the Wright brothers released new forces and it is our essential task to direct these forces into constructive channels. The record of past achievement contains indispensable guides to future endeavor. In our failures there is a challenge to discover new avenues of creative effort. A decade ago we dreamed briefly of a parliament of man. The dream was followed by an unhappy awakening in which mere political internationalism became, for the time at least, a discredited panacea. It was discovered that problems of armaments, finance, population, raw materials, trade, and prestige are economic, social, or even psychological, rather than political, and that the political devices of coöperation can be no more than tools with which we may come to grips with more fundamental factors. On all sides, there are heartening indications of a growing awareness of these fundamental truths and of a renewed determination to build a more enduring order for the great community.

The genius of mankind for construction, far from being an exhausted resource, has only begun to disclose its potential powers. Experience has taught us that we are capable of building still more bravely. If the shell-shocked leaders of the war generation cannot bring social engineering abreast of contemporary need, they must be put aside for leaders of clearer vision and more resolute determination. The reverts who strut their little time upon the stage may recall George Canning's "wholesome state" of international relations, when it was "every nation for itself and God for us all." The work of builders may be retarded, but sooner or later the relentless advance of constructive effort will be resumed. We shall take command of the "zero hour" and make of it the daybreak of a renewed progress.

SOCIALISM IN RELATION TO WAR AND PEACE

CARL LANDAUER

PROFESSOR OF ECONOMICS
IN THE UNIVERSITY OF CALIFORNIA

Lecture delivered September 29, 1937

SOCIALISM IN RELATION TO
WAR AND PEACE

THE TOPIC of "socialism in its relation to war and peace" covers two great problems. One of them refers to the future and may be expressed by the question: Will a socialist society, if it is ever created, be more peaceful than the present-day capitalistic society? The second is a historian's problem, and it may be formulated thus: What has the socialist movement contributed to the cause of peace?

There is a well-known theory which says that capitalism alone is responsible for the menace of war in modern society. In its crude form this theory suggests that all wars are fought in the interests of the capitalists. When we survey history it is easy to find some wars which were really fought in the economic interest of a small but powerful minority; but the proposition becomes entirely unconvincing if applied to the great national wars of modern times, and to the wars which threaten to break out in our own day. As a business proposition, modern war is very unattractive; even the munitions industries proper, which form only a very small part of the total industry in any modern country, have more to gain from strong armament than from actual war. If the decision between war and peace were made on a dollars and cents basis, peace would be safe.

There is a more developed form of the same theory, and it does not picture war as a rational undertaking of capitalists to increase their profits, but as an act of despair to which capitalism resorts in its period of decay. While even in this form the theory is not convincing, it can make us realize a very important fact. War is indeed a product of irrational emotions, and despair has an important place among them. I do not think that this despair has ever been confined to the capitalists. But the feeling of economic frustration is certainly one of the reasons why peoples may resort to war.

Whoever tries to list the causes of war in the present age will have to include these items in his list: lust for power, racial hatred, and the desire for self-assertion on the part of nations whose self-confidence has been badly shaken. None of these motives is likely to disappear automatically with a change of the economic system. But the probability of war does not alone depend on the existence of conscious motives which may lead statesmen to aggressive action. Those motives may very well be kept under control, like asocial motives in the national community, if prevailing habits of thought are not favorable to them but strengthen the counteracting motives for order and peace. Our habits of thought, however, are greatly influenced by the kind of economic system under which we live. If we are accustomed to think of our fellow humans as our natural collaborators, we shall resist the forces which are apt to make us their foes; if we think of them primarily as our economic rivals, we shall be inclined to let ourselves be drawn into an attitude of hostility. The capitalistic system does not emphasize the necessity of coöperation. To be sure, every economic system, and therefore capitalism too, is at bottom a system of coöperation. But in capitalism coöperation is organized through competition. The early philosophers of laissez faire praised the wisdom of an economic system in which an unseen hand guided the individuals to do what was best for society while each of them was only conscious of doing what was good for himself, in a struggle with other individuals. These philosophers judged capitalism only by its performance as an economic machine; but an economic system is a mode of living, and therefore its performance in production is not all that counts. The psychological effects through which the system obtains its practical results are important, too. Capitalism educates men to look at their fellow men as competitors rather than collaborators, and a competitor is a foe. In this way capitalism forms habits of thought which are dangerous for human society, and particularly dangerous for international peace. Let me illustrate by reference to the most important example which history has offered us. I think it is absurd to believe that the World War broke out because the English capitalists considered it a profitable project to destroy their German competitors by means of war, or because the German capitalists believed that the gains from any conquered colony would offset the losses of a war. But very few observers, if any, will deny that the World War would not have been possible but for the mistrust, the fear, and the hatred among nations which had grown out of industrial competition. Certainly these feelings had other roots, too; but it would in all probability have been possible to keep them under control if the nations, and particularly the British and the Germans, had not acquired the habit of looking at each other as bitter rivals in their daily lives.

Of course, man must live, and if capitalism were the only economic order which could afford us the means of living, we would have to accept its undesirable traits. This is not the occasion to discuss the problem of how the economic order can be reformed. Some of us may be more, others less optimistic with regard to the promise of existing reform movements. But certainly a majority of those interested in the development of society agree on two things: First, that in the course of decades or centuries mankind will very likely find a better economic system than present-day capitalism; even a superficial survey of social changes in the past suggests the idea that capitalism, or at least the present form of capitalism, will hardly be the final form of economic life. Second, that the society of the future, whatever its other characteristics, will impose more economic responsibilities on public bodies than these bodies have in our present economy. This process means increased importance of coöperation and decreased importance of competition. If it will be possible to carry the process on to the establishment of a socialistic order—as I think it will—the change will detract so much from the disposition of nations to war as to make war highly improbable; but even an approach to socialism will greatly increase the chances of peace.

However, all this is long-range policy. An economic change cannot be accomplished rapidly, and certainly not if it is to be accomplished by peaceful means; and while we need not wait for the final result to see some effects on habits of thought, every phase in the development of laws and institutions will take time to change those habits. The socialists have had to realize that mankind cannot afford to wait for economic change to reduce the danger of war, otherwise mankind might be wiped out before it could ever see socialism. Most socialists saw clearly that they had to work for peace in the existing capitalistic society.

In this country pacifist sentiment has always been strong among people of almost all political beliefs. It is therefore difficult for Americans to realize that in most European countries the socialist movement has always been by far the greatest single force working for peace.

The part of the socialists in the promotion of the peace idea has been so conspicuous that some further explanation should be made, here, of why they gave so much of their strength to this task. Socialism is, after all, primarily a movement with economic aims, and on the surface of it there seems to be hardly more reason for a socialist to be a peace lover than for any other reasonable and well-intentioned person. Why have socialists taken the lead in the struggle for peace?

We sometimes hear this answer: Because the worker has no fatherland. The socialist, if he is not himself a worker, is a sympathizer with the working class; therefore he also should reject the idea of a fatherland. But the huge majority of the workers in all countries have never felt that they had no fatherland. They have loved their country and made sacrifices for its sake even when it treated them badly. By expressing their belief in internationalism the majority of workers and socialists in every country have never meant to say that they were disinterested in the fate of their nation, but that all nations depend on each other and should live together in brotherhood.

The reason why the socialist movement became thoroughly interested in peace lies in the fact that socialism is only a means to an end, and the end, as a socialist sees it, is a better life for mankind. If the term 'humanitarian' were not tied up with the connotation of benevolence rather than of self-reliance and ethical responsibility, we could very appropriately call socialism the greatest humanitarian movement in the modern world.

The socialist movement as a whole has never made the mistake which individual socialists (not Karl Marx) have made, namely, to disregard all the noneconomic aspects of human life. Socialism has interested itself in a number of demands which were not very closely connected with its economic program; I need mention only the legal position of women, or the modernization of educational systems, or fair treatment of racial minorities. The reason why socialism concerned itself with these issues was the realization that economic progress can be made much more valuable if it is supplemented by progress in other fields of human endeavor, and that the results of economic progress can be jeopardized if improvements in other fields are not forthcoming. This consideration is never more justified than when we deal with the problem of peace. What would be the use of improving the economic system if men were doomed to kill each other off with shells and poison gas?

From the great number of documents which express the motives of the great socialist parties in their work for peace and their attitude toward the problem of nationality and internationalism, I want to quote a few sentences from the program of the French Socialist Party, adopted at the Congress of Tours in 1902. At that time the party already included the large majority of the rank and file as well as of the socialist deputies, though not all French socialists, and it was under the leadership of the great socialist and internationalist, Jean Jaurès, who on the eve of the World War was assassinated by a war-crazy superpatriot. "It would be useless," we read in the program, "to prepare inside each nation an organization of justice and peace, if the relations of the nations to one another remained exposed to every enterprise of force, every suggestion of capitalist greed. The Socialist Party desires peace among nations.... It wishes to protect the territory and the independence of the nation against any surprise; but every offensive policy and offensive weapon is utterly condemned by it." In a later passage the program pictures the society of the future and says that "the difference of classes will have disappeared, and the difference of nations, instead of being a principle of strife and hatred, will be a principle of brotherly emulation in the universal progress of mankind."

In the last two decades before the war, there was only one other man who had as authoritative a position in the International as Jean Jaurès, and this was the German socialist August Bebel. He expressed his opinion on nationality and internationalism many times, and in spite of some disagreement over means and tactics, there was complete unity in principle between him and Jaurès. I want to give you one of his statements, which he made before the National Convention of the German Social Democratic Party in 1907. This statement does not express the basic philosophy of socialism on international relations, for which Bebel found excellent words on other occasions, but it gives a very characteristic interpretation of the value of national independence from a socialist's standpoint: "If ever we must defend our country, then we shall defend it because it is our country, because it is the land in which we live, the land whose language we speak, whose customs are ours, and because we want to make this fatherland a more perfect and beautiful country than exists anywhere else in the world. Therefore we will not defend our fatherland for the sake of the capitalists but in spite of the capitalists."

To be sure, these statements do not represent the unanimous opinion of the socialists, either in prewar or in postwar days. There has always been a wing of radical antipatriots who did not acknowledge that the proletariat has any interest in the existence of separate nations; previous to the war Hervé—later an extreme nationalist—in France was the most influential spokesman for this wing; in Germany, Karl Liebknecht advocated the same view in a somewhat milder form. There was a wing which believed war to be absolutely inevitable in a capitalistic society, and therefore peace propaganda under capitalism entirely futile; the Frenchman Longuet represented this group. Finally, there were a number of right-wing reformists, like the Germans Ludwig Quessel and Karl Hildebrandt, who came perilously near to a nationalistic philosophy. But all these dissenters had a very small following, as compared with the great socialist membership and the socialist vote in the large European countries.

Thus the socialist masses, previous to the World War, were

committed to two ideas about international life: the rejection of war as a means of settling international disputes, and the affirmation of the value of national independence and self-determination for all peoples, large and small. We must keep this in mind when we want to understand the attitude of the socialists during the World War. War came into a world in which socialism was already powerful but not powerful enough to determine the destinies of the nations. There was not one single socialist in any of the European cabinets when the World War broke out. Up to the very eve of the war the socialists fought the policies of those in high positions who wanted war or were not active enough to prevent war. But the efforts were of no avail; war came, and the socialists had to face a dilemma which their most farsighted leaders had always feared: they either had to participate in warfare, or they had to deliver their country to the mercy, not of the socialists, but of the militarists of the opposite side.

What happened to socialism in 1914 was a defeat, but it was not a betrayal. It is the privilege of any observer to argue that the defeat could have been avoided by better strategy, or by the display of more energy or courage. Some of us may believe that the effects of the failure to prevent war could have been diminished if the socialists had decided to refrain from any participation in the conduct of war, though it would necessarily have lead to the immediate victory of the country where socialists were least powerful; one may argue that this triumph of violence would not have been lasting, or even that the refusal of socialists would have had such a propaganda effect as to instigate a general strike of all armies. Finally, there may be people who think the world is so bad now that it could not have been worse if the socialists had accepted the risk of defeating their own nations; the violent groups seem to dominate international politics anyway, and a socialist refusal to take up arms or to work on munitions, or to vote for war credits, or to pay war taxes, would at least have been a profession of faith. None of these ways of reasoning has seemed to me, personally, convincing; but I am far from suggesting that the case is closed. However, while we may raise the question whether the socialists should have made a different decision from that which nearly all of them made at the outbreak of the war, we shall have to acknowledge that the dilemma which they saw really existed. It is a widely held opinion that the European socialists, with the exception of Karl Liebknecht and a few men of the Independent Labor Party in England, were either too cowardly or were carried away by emotions contrary to their faith, and therefore did not follow their socialist convictions in August, 1914. But it seems to me that anyone who has gone through the records of those days must get a very different picture indeed.

The war, in its later phase, split the socialist movement. The terrific sacrifices in terms of all values of civilization horrified a good number of socialists so much that they felt compelled to make at least a profession of faith against the frustration of human reason and the destruction of material as well as ethical standards; others, not less desirous of ending the war, sought to accomplish it by political action within the framework of national politics and in the meantime continued their support of national defense. This, however, was not a permanent split; when the war was over, it became clear that the war issue itself, though of vital importance during the conflict, was not caused by a disagreement over ends or principles, but by a controversy about means. Another split within the ranks of socialism was lasting. It was not caused by the war itself, but by the fact that the war greatly increased the influence of socialism on governments and therefore raised some fundamental questions concerning the use of that new power. The cleavage between the absolute pacifists in the socialist movement and those socialists who tried to work for peace while not rejecting national defense was quickly healed, but the split between these two groups and the communists proved lasting.

Socialism not only lost the struggle against war in July, 1914; it also lost its struggle for a negotiated peace. War was carried on until one side was entirely defeated, and then an unjust and cruel peace was imposed on the nations which had lost the war. However, this second defeat, which socialism shared with the Catholic Church and with Wilsonian liberalism, became a source of strength. The militarists had overruled the socialists, but this had not made the world feel any better. International understanding seemed more necessary than ever, and the socialists recognized the great task. Just as in prewar days, they became the great force working for peace. The fact that in this period, more at any rate than before the war, they could enlist the support of other groups did not detract from their importance as the center of the peace movement in Europe. Neither Briand's nor Stresemann's policy would have been possible without the support of the socialists. For Stresemann, who was very much opposed to the economic philosophy of socialism, this led to a personal and political tragedy. Whenever an attempt was made to strengthen the League of Nations, as, for example, the Geneva Protocol of 1924, or to secure peace through special treaties, as, for example, the Locarno Pact, the socialists were either the authors of that policy or at least its main defenders in their own countries.

This work for peace was greatly facilitated by the fact that the socialist parties of the various belligerent countries reestablished their own alliance very quickly when war was over. Preliminary conferences began within a few months after the armistice, and in the summer of 1920 a general congress of the International was held in Geneva. To be sure, not all the bad feeling disappeared when the delegates from Germany met with the British and French and Belgian socialists; for some time the Germans felt that the Western socialists were not active enough in their attempts to change the Versailles treaty, and the French and Belgian and, to a less degree, the English socialists felt that the Germans were not sufficiently willing to denounce the unjustifiable acts of the Imperial régime; it is also true that in the Western countries, where the enthusiasm created by the military victory had thoroughly permeated the masses, war psychology still dominated the rank and file at a time when the leaders were already engaged in friendly talks with their German comrades. However, the restoration of the International immediately after the war proved that warlike emotions had not killed the will for international solidarity in the hearts of the socialists, and this was a fact of fundamental importance and great practical value.

While there is no good reason to question either the sincerity or the energy of the socialists in their work for peace since 1918, they have certainly been guilty of one great mistake. This mistake was not theirs alone; it was the mistake of very nearly the whole peace movement. With very few exceptions, they overestimated the moral effect of an international peace organization and underrated the necessity of taking definite measures against aggressors. They gave too much weight to the danger that any defensive alliance, as well as the provisions for sanctions in the League's Covenant, might be misused for aggressive purposes, and too little weight to the danger that a peaceful nation or the entire League might be helpless in the face of an act of open aggression. It is easy to understand what caused this mistake, but explanation does not make it less disastrous.

We have reviewed the positive aspects of socialism in its relation to peace; but is there not a negative side too? Socialism is connected, historically and to some degree theoretically, with the idea of the class struggle. Is this idea not contradictory to peace within a nation, and may it not even endanger international peace?

When we say 'peace' we do not, of course, mean absence of struggle; else we would better say 'death'. Peace in the sense in which it is reconcilable with life means not elimination but limitation of struggle; it means an order which excludes violent means but permits and even encourages competition of conflicting ideas and interests. Every realistically minded person must see that there are conflicts of interests between social groups—whether or not we want to call them classes is largely a matter of taste. The struggle between the social groups is inevitable; not to oppress it, but to keep it within the limits of peacefulness, is possible and necessary. The socialist movement of all the great Western countries has accepted the idea of limiting the class struggle. Russia is the only great country where those who want a socialist society are willing to use force and oppression for its establishment.

However, this does not mean that in the rest of the world socialism can never become the objective of violent struggle. There is no human aspiration which cannot become a cause of war, either civil or international, and socialism is certainly no exception. In a democratic society everybody who wants a change is under an obligation to work for this change only through the machinery of constituted government, and no person or group, however important and desirable its aims, is exempt from this obligation. But if a group obeys the rules on which peaceful society is founded, it has a right to be protected, or to protect itself; if its opponents try to suppress it by violence, the group is entitled to meet force with force. If the opponents of socialism resort to arms to build up a dictatorship, the socialists have a right to fight for their cause, and if they have a fair chance of success it is their duty to fight rather than to surrender.

But for socialism the necessity of using violence means in itself partial failure, even if violence is used only in defense and successfully. Violence is contrary to the motives for socialism, and neither the actual violence of civil or international war nor the potential violence of a firmly established dictatorship is a suitable environment for that work of economic rebuilding which socialism wants to do. As long as nations are in something like a normal state of mind, the danger that the issue of socialism leads to a break in the order of national or international peace is fortunately small; those who want to resist any change in their socially privileged position by means of force, as well as those who want to speed up the process by violence, isolate themselves from the mass of the nation because the people at large, though divided by differences of opinion and interest, are unanimous in their appreciation of peace. This simple fact is the reason why fascists and communists alike have been disappointed again and again in their expectation of a collapse of democracy in the Western countries, or of a war between the "bourgeois democracies" and the proletarian Soviet republic.

However, the case is entirely different if a nation loses its natural mental equilibrium and if therefore hatred and impatience are no longer balanced by abhorrence of violence. In such an abnormal state of mind the motives of hostility are even strengthened by that mystical belief in the blessing of strong-hand methods which grows so easily out of despair and shattered self-reliance. This is what happened in the fascist countries. Those who explain fascism simply as a result of the class struggle stop at a point where the most interesting part of the explanation would have to start. Certainly, class antagonisms have much to do with the origin of fascism and with the resulting oppression and threat of war. But the existence of class antagonisms is a very normal situation.

What is abnormal is only the weakness of the integrating elements in the national and international community, of the natural sentiment which ordinarily tells the common man that there is seldom a victory which is worth a war, and that acts of ruthlessness are likely to do more damage than can be remedied even by a great success. Because this sentiment has become weak in some nations, fascism exists and threatens to spread destruction.

Since we have to face this fact now, what can we do about it? Some people seem to think that one should never raise issues which might cause struggle, since any struggle might develop into civil strife and ultimately into war. Certainly, if we did not have a movement for socialism we would have one issue less which could endanger peace.

Let us make every effort to do some clear thinking about this vital question. It may very well be that no individual reform, proposed either by socialists or nonsocialists, is worth the destruction caused by any violence. Should we therefore silence the reformers, or forget thinking about reforms? Nobody has yet frankly suggested such a course, but the talk and the actions of a good number of people betray the belief that if we can maintain peace only by preserving society exactly as it is, we should accept this condition.

But this is a price which we cannot pay even for peace. Let us always keep in mind that violent action in the offensive is never justified by the importance of any goal, and that even in the defensive, violence is so destructive that large sacrifices in terms of speed of progress are justifiable and necessary if they serve the cause of peace. Nobody's pet ideas are worth fighting for, even if they are good in themselves. But one thing is worth fighting for, namely, the possibility of change, the existence of a social machinery which provides means to adjust institutions to changing conditions. Even peace is only a means to preserve life, and life requires change. Whoever tries to destroy the machinery for change becomes an outlaw. We should try to change his attitude by persuasion. But if we do not succeed, we shall have to treat him as an outlaw. The existence of a machinery for peaceful change is one of the very few things which are really worth every sacrifice, and any attempt to maintain peace without a machinery for social change will inevitably remain futile.

FASCISM IN RELATION TO
WAR AND PEACE

———

ROBERT A. BRADY

ASSOCIATE PROFESSOR OF ECONOMICS
IN THE UNIVERSITY OF CALIFORNIA

Lecture delivered October 6, 1937

FASCISM IN RELATION TO
WAR AND PEACE

Fascism may be briefly defined as a political system representing the effort of a vested and self-confessed hereditary "élite" to rivet its social-economic controls through establishment of permanent servile status for the mass of the population. In it plutocracy commands the machinery of state for promotion of the conditions of fixity of status, fixity of occupation, and fixity of residence for all members of society below the level of the ruling class. The effect is to crystallize lines of class cleavage, and so to adjust the resultant graded hierarchy of "wealth and talents" as to render vertical mobility difficult if not impossible, and to freeze social lines to the point where they shade imperceptibly into caste.

These patterns are brought to focus in the formula of the "corporate state," and are given some degree of theoretical content in three basic principles, namely, the "leader" principle, the "authority" principle, and the "total" principle. The paired sanctions upon which these rest are throughout antidemocratic, antiliberal, and antiequalitarian. They are, consequently, antirational. But in giving rise to what its spokesmen so happily term "myths," "cults," and "fanatical loyalties," these may be taken to represent no more than apt characterization of the mood of Fascism's adroitly compounded propaganda for the interest deflection of the masses, and as a barrage behind which to construct elaborate sets of fully implemented and thoroughly despotic controls. The controls established are best described as those found necessary in any given current national environment in order most adequately to buttress the ramparts of monopoly-oriented capitalism faced with impending mass revolt.

That is, Fascism is Janus-faced, one face looking toward "spiritual values," the other toward "material values." The first-named values comprise the manna for its general public; the second trace the lines of vested interest and guide the helm of *Realpolitik*. The first are charismatic, with grace centered in the national state and vocalized in patriotic fanaticism. The second are matter-of-fact, with power funneled through the machinery of state and control over the general population actualized in de facto militarization of all social-economic relations.

Both the particular machinery and the involutions of propaganda may vary with peculiarities of social and economic organization, historical background, national traditions, international position, and similar factors. But these condition the expression, not the direction; the effectiveness, not the purposes, of Fascism. The systems of Fascist Italy and Nazi Germany, in short, are born of the same coagulation of interests, are designed to serve the same functions, are sketched out with reference to a common set of challenges, and are guided to the same general ends. Their programs vary endlessly in detail and in effectiveness, but not in fundamental structure nor in dominating mood. And the same holds to some degree both in all other *Fascist-oriented* states, such as Portugal, Austria, Poland, Hungary, Greece, and Japan, and with the unfolding of *Fascist-inclined* elements in all liberal-democratic states such as our own, England, and France.

So to characterize Fascism means to take sharp issue with all those authorities who describe that system as the peculiar product of Italian conditions and who, in drawing a line between Fascism and Nazism, find the common elements in both peculiar to the conditions uniquely common to the two nations. This latter view, which has, incidentally, been expressly repudiated by both Mussolini and Hitler, is most cogently summarized in von Beckerath's article on Fascism in the *Encyclopaedia of the Social Sciences*. "It is only when viewed as a peculiarly Italian phenomenon," he writes, "that the essence of Fascism becomes clearly delineated." He continues: "In its philosophy, its origins and development, its political structure and cultural aspirations, it is an integral part of the Italian matrix. The ideology of Fascism viewed historico-genetically is a peculiar fusion of syndicalist theory and the doctrines of Italian nationalism."

So long as von Beckerath confines his attention to the peculiarities of Italian Fascism his position is certainly correct. But to speak of Fascism as the product of the Italian national system on any other basis is to misunderstand completely the phenomena he has set himself to describe. Of course, one may object that the particular word, "fascism," being derived as a figure from the ancient Roman *fasces* or bundle of rods symbolizing Roman imperial authority, can only properly be applied in Italy. It is not, however, the origin of the symbol which determines the freedom with which it can be employed, but rather the veracity with which the term summarizes a common process, or represents a uniform set of elements. Since the structures, drives, and objectives lying at the heart of Italian Fascism are in no wise unique, but are rather to be found in some form or other in all countries organized on a highly developed capitalistic footing, the more general use of the term—not by analogy, but by analysis—is fully justified. Careful investigation, for example, will show no striking differences between the system of Italy and that of Germany, beyond those found in certain features of formal structure.

There are three mutually complementary ways to demonstrate the adequacy of this view; namely, by examination (1) of achievements, (2) of structure, and (3) of theories advanced by spokesmen. These can then be examined in the light of certain long-run trends, checked against interpretations based upon an insufficient grasp of the rudiments of the Fascist outlook, and appraised in terms of the implications they carry for the future of war and peace. This is the procedure which will be followed in the rest of this discussion—a procedure which frankly relegates Fascist theories to a subordinate position behind the fact-parade of Fascist practice in explanation of the leading drives of the systems devised.

It is the beginning of wisdom to understand at the very outset that in those countries whose national systems are fully laid out along Fascist lines none of the elements considered basic to capitalistic enterprise have been disturbed at any key point or in any significant fashion. Thus, economic life is organized, as before, uniformly on a profit-making basis, decisions in all matters relating to the conduct of enterprise rest with the employer, and the results are gauged in terms of individual or corporate profit-and-loss accounts. Private property in the means of production has been solemnly affirmed, the sanctity of individual contracts upheld, and whatever measures of laissez faire or free competition are considered necessary at any given point by the business community are maintained.

Nor has any of the usual business machinery been scrapped or radically overhauled. Thus the corporation, with its accredited representatives and its lists of stock- and bondholders, is ubiquitous. Trade associations, cartels, interlocking directorates, financial consortiums, stock and commodity exchanges exist and function much as before the advent of Fascism. None of the big trusts has been broken up in either the heavy or the light industries, and no obstacles have been placed in the way of vertical and horizontal combination, pooling of patents, uniform price agreements, establishment of production quotas, or other devices servant to the expansion of ever more widely ranging business empire.

On the contrary,—and this point is of key importance to an understanding of Fascism as here discussed,—collusive action via trade associations, combinations, cartels, chambers of commerce, industrial associations, and numerous other forms has been rendered simpler, easier, and more general. The formula under which such business expansion proceeds in both Italy and Germany has been made familiar to Americans in the phrase, "self-government in business." This formula provides a leitmotiv running through all Fascist literature, and, as in NRA, such "self-government" has in reality meant not increased governmental interference in the business system, but wholesale abdication of government from regulation of it. At the same time it lends to strategically placed special-interest blocs legal and quasi legal powers to enforce decisions on recalcitrant minorities. Typically, the business associations are run entirely and throughout of, by, and for the interest of dominant blocs without regard to either small-business men or the economic status of the labor and salaried classes. In fact, this is so generally taken for granted that well-informed German business men interviewed in 1935 and 1936 regarded NRA as of essentially the same pattern as that achieved in Germany through the benefactions of the Third Reich. And in this view (except only so far as Art. 7-A is concerned) they are substantially correct.

The gains via Fascism to business consolidations at the peak of the economic pyramid do not end with mere sweeping away of barriers to exercise of effective monopoly powers. Whereas under the old régime government assumed a largely passive rôle, acting as umpire in the pursuit of business ends according to the accepted competitive rules, under the new system its forces are mobilized and directed as required by exigencies of monopolistic strategy. Thus the government has been brought to deploy its forces in guaranty of the right of the business community to fix prices, limit production, prevent the coming in of new competitors, limit machine hours and plant schedules, and so forth. The various so-called "self-governing" bodies which dominate current Italian and German business enterprise are, in this respect, autonomous functional units within the framework of a political system spun and operated on its own behalf.

Moreover, the bulk of the public works and military programs are advocated, built up, and carried out on a basis of promotion of business advantage. No clear line can be drawn here between normal public works and armanent programs, nor between home and foreign policy. Arguments advanced are clear, unambiguous, and to the point. Public works give aid to construction industries; to cement, brick, and furniture industries; bring new land into cultivation, and protect foreign exchanges. Armaments keep fuel, metal-refining, machine and allied industries operating at or near capacity and on a satisfactory profit basis.

That is not to say that in any simple and direct fashion armaments and the heavy industries control the government. Such is not the fact. Rather it is to say that under a system combining the economic dictatorship of monopoly-tending capitalism with the cramping confines of the national state, the business-controlled government is willy-nilly driven to promote the deployment of economic resources in this fashion. Circumstances being such as they are in Fascist states, there is no good alternative to a continuation of such support. It is, for example, perfectly safe to say that if, for any reason whatsoever, the armaments programs of Germany and Italy were to be cut off sharply, both countries would experience quick and disastrous economic collapse. And by the same token, any considerable lightening of the burden of armaments would be paced if not exceeded by a business recession of serious proportions.

There are other aspects of Fascist militarization which promote this particular channeling of public aid, to which I shall return a bit later. But it is worth noting here that the drive behind armaments is, in these respects, no different from the drives utilized to promote public works activities during depression times or periods of unusual stress in general. The ancient Egyptians built pyramids; the Roman emperors constructed public buildings and rebuilt the city; moderns build dams, subsidize railroad rebuilding, or go in heavily for armaments. Thereby key feeder industries are improved, plant capacity ratings are bettered, and minimum-profit margins assured. That the net economic advantage to the country at large may be less than nil does not matter. For example, none of the large-scale business executives interviewed in Germany would have objected, so far as the strictly business side of the picture is concerned, had all the steel been dumped into the North Sea instead of congealed into the instrumentalities of war. Their returns are conditioned not on use, but on production schedules and price levels. Under the circumstances it was expedient to employ productive resources for armament, and for obvious reasons it was no more politically feasible to use public funds to produce steel for sea burial than it would have been for President Roosevelt to propose construction of a pons asinorum across the Pacific in 1933—though subsequently, under our new dispensation, much else was proposed and carried out that was qualitatively not far removed.

Finally, the Fascist foreign program looks toward full mobilization of the resources of the state behind the interests of its nationals in concessions, markets, shipping, and general expansion abroad. It does this not on behalf of the state, but on behalf of business enterprise. Even a most casual examination of the arguments, the plans, and the point of view as expressed in the day-by-day literature concerning such matters will convince the most skeptical of the truth of this statement. The powers of the state under Fascism are employed here in the same mood and are servant to the same parallelogram of forces as those which dominate in the making of tariffs and the granting of subsidies. The rôle played by the state is strictly analogous to that of mercantilist times. To be sure, many eminent historians, not least among them the famous Swedish economist and author of two huge volumes on mercantilism, Eli Heckscher, have spoken of mercantilist tactics as subordinate to enhancement of the power of the state. But even Heckscher is clear that the leading functions which such enhanced power was to perform, were centered around the task of clearing away internal barriers to trade and industry, on the one hand, and promotion of the economic interests of nationals abroad, on the other. Such is unequivocally and even more emphatically true of the Fascist systems of Italy and Germany. To reverse the line of emphasis is to be classed with the naïve and the credulous on the sucker list of ambidextrous public relations counselors who write Fascist propaganda, as well as to confess ignorance of the elementary facts of Fascist *Realpolitik*.

To summarize briefly at this point: In both Italy and Germany, (1) the entirety of capitalistic institutions and methods has been maintained; (2) the government has smoothed the way for concentration of economic power in fewer and fewer hands, and throws its support wholeheartedly on the side of monopoly; (3) the system of organization is known as "self-government in business," and allows participants practically free reign in collusion; (4) the state assembles resources for programs of public works and armaments building without which the heavy industries would be bankrupt and profitless; and (5) these armaments are employed to secure economic concessions and to promote economic expansion abroad.

All this does not mean, of course, that under Fascism the business community is satisfied. In general, small-business men, competing in any fashion with large concerns, are being harmed and pushed to the wall. Whether competing or not, small concerns do not possess the power to prevent an undue proportion of the burdens involved in financing the new system from being shifted onto their shoulders. Between high prices, with consequent shrinkage of mass purchasing power, and the tax collector, the petty bourgeoisie are being squeezed to the limits of endurance. In general, the little-business man is being crushed.

Moreover, the big concerns are not necessarily satisfied. The question arises, Where is the money required for the public works and armaments coming from? Part of it may come out of the increased volume of activity per se; part of it by way of redistribution of wealth and income. Both sources are being tapped. On the one hand, the standard of living of the general population is being held constant or actually depressed; on the other, business is being asked to surrender a proportion of returns, required in order (1) to finance the system of control devised to promote business interests at home and abroad, and (2) to continue subsidy of public works and armaments on which business prosperity rests. Business complaints about partial surrender of such receipts, however, are to be interpreted in the same light as those of persons who buy tax-exempt government bonds in order to evade the tax collector at the same time that they campaign against high taxes devised to collect money in order to pay for projects out of which the money used to purchase the tax-exempt bonds was originally made. This is not disapproval of government, nor of the devices of a particular government; it is a desire to escape the incidence of its cost upon oneself or one's business.

So much for the strictly business side of the Fascist picture. The obverse side, that affecting labor, the peasants, and the professional class, is even more significant for the purposes of this discussion. In the large it is not difficult to summarize this side of the ledger, for the leading facts are simple, easy to get at, and unambiguously clear. Labor and the peasantry have been forced to still lower economic levels than before the advent of the Fascists, their organizations for defense of group interests destroyed, and their future rendered well-nigh hopeless. The professional class has been coördinated to a propaganda machine corrosive of the very elementary determinants for vitality in the arts and sciences, the intellectual level of schools and universities has been undermined, and all tenures have become insecure.

It is a fair deduction from the history, theory, and practice of Fascism that the gravamen of its attack was the threat of mass revolt against what had become well-nigh intolerable conditions in the lower income brackets. The combination of elements behind it was reactionary in the extreme; the mood and direction of its drive were unmistakable. Mussolini's "march on Rome" began at Milan, the industrial center of northern Italy and a headquarters for commercialized agriculture and the owners of the great *latifundia*. The elements united under his banner consisted, on the one hand, of industrial, commercial, and financial interests of the cities and medium-sized and large farming interests, and on the other, a medley of rootless and confused petty bourgeois, youngsters thrown prematurely on the unemployment market and without any prospect of occupation for an indefinite period of time to come, jobless ex-service men, and a fringe of unscrupulous labor leaders willing to deny their following for the promises of office and a chance at party emoluments.

Much the same combination was found in Germany. On the one hand, the Junkers, Ruhr industrialists, and the great banking and commercial houses; on the other, unemployed clerks, bankrupt little-business men, officers from the ex-service ranks, futureless university students, some of the *lumpen* proletariat, a fringe of the middle-class farmers, and many of the unemployed. Wherever one goes, Fascist forces are found blended of the same elements. In Spain, they are the decadent grandees of the Riviera, the upper hierarchy of the Church, the heads of the great commercial, financial, and industrial houses, royalist sympathizers, the officer staff of the military, and adventurers at large. The same holds for Greece, Portugal, Hungary, and Poland.

The "march on Rome" was made in Pullman coaches, and the bills were paid by the "Liberty Leaguers" of the industrial north. Hitler made his trips into the Ruhr in 1929 and 1930, and he assumed power with the guaranteed support of the

Junkers and their allies within the Federation of German Industries and similar groups. The popular following of both Mussolini and Hitler was whipped up out of dissident elements in general and used by ambidextrous demagogues to spread terror among the ranks of labor and to serve as vigilantes in the countryside.

To this end, union headquarters were systematically raided, labor papers destroyed, labor meetings broken up, the poorer peasantry terrorized, the coöperatives boycotted, all liberal sentiment in the schools, the press, or elsewhere obliterated, and a supine and frequently conniving police defied. (It may seem a pretty difficult dose for us to swallow, but it is nevertheless true that we see here no more than a large-scale European version of the combination familiar to Americans in prohibition days, of the "beer ring and the racketeer"—only that the "beer ring" has hired some high-class public relations counselors to write its deceptive propaganda, and the "racketeer" has turned political and learned to organize his vigilante squads into a national system.) The terrorism was justified on the basis of "law and order" and on behalf of "truth and justice." It was advertised as patriotism to traditions, fatherland, the flag, the rights of property, and as the eternal enemy of democracy, liberalism, and doctrines of equal rights and opportunities.

The results have been pretty much as might be expected. In both countries all semblance of democratic institutions has been destroyed. Labor unions have been abolished, their leaders dispersed, placed in concentration camps, or executed, and their funds confiscated. Their papers have been taken over, their political parties banned, and their right to expression of opinion in press, forum, radio, or elsewhere denied. All lower peasant and rural labor organizations, federations, and associations have suffered the same fate. In both countries the functions of all labor and peasant organizations have been taken over by associations knit into a gigantic, nation-wide, "company-union" network, controlled from on top and completely subservient to employer interests.

The product of this has been lower wages, longer hours, poorer working conditions, higher costs of living. The official figures allow no escape from this conclusion. Much is made out of certain supplementary services, such as the vacation trips of *Kraft durch Freude,* the theatrical arts programs of this organization and *Dopolavoro,* and provision of medical clinics. These are not, however, supplied free of cost, as is generally advertised, but are paid for out of deductions from labor income, and at a rate sufficient to pay for the services entirely, plus party overhead charged to such functions.

Nor, moreover, do the official pronouncements of governmental officials deny that the status of persons in the lower income brackets has not been improved in material terms. No footnotes are required for the statement by Ley, Leader of the Labor Front, in his speech of March, 1935, where he says: "We could not offer the working masses any material benefits, for Germany was poor and in a state of confusion and misery. New rates or wages and similar things were out of the question." Hence, it was necessary to "suppress the materialism" which gave rise to demands for improved standards of living, and "instead divert the gaze of the workers to the spiritual values of the nation." It is only a short step from this to Goering's cynical remark, that what Germany requires is "cannon instead of butter."

Aside from thus causing the people in lower income brackets to substitute "cannon" and "spiritual values" for victuals, both governments say they have benefited labor through elimination of unemployment. To this assertion, the following remarks are relevant: (1) From the unemployed rolls have been struck all "enemies of the state,"—persons defined as socialists, communists, trade-union leaders (plus, in Germany, aliens and Jews),—all those not on the registry rolls from having been unemployed too long, all women who can lay claim to a breadwinner by first of kin, all those included in the army, navy, aviation services, labor camps, rural services, and the official parties as active workers, and all those who have a plot of ground large enough to supply part of the family table. (2) Those finding employment through government programs receive approximately relief wages, some of them—notably in the labor camps—less than relief wages. (3) The wages received are taxed with various types of official deductions, and various so-called "voluntary contributions." The latter are typically either taken off pay rolls, or are rendered unavoidable through pressures of one sort or another. In a large business office in Berlin, it was estimated that these deductions constitute from one-fifth to one-third of the income of the entire office staff. When it is remembered that, with a cost of living approximately as high as that in the United States at present, a highly skilled workman in a German machine shop draws a maximum of 247 marks per month,—or slightly under $100,—the significance of such deductions can be appreciated. Deductions in Italy appear to be of about the same proportion. (4) In both Germany and Italy the quality of many products has gone down through the forced sale of substitute (*Ersatz*) goods.

The situation of the peasantry in the two countries is even worse. Arthur Feiler, writing a series of articles for the *Frankfurter Zeitung* in the winter of 1930, compared the position of the German peasant to the status of his predecessor at the time of the savage Peasant Wars in the early sixteenth century. Unquestionably, almost irrespective of the aspect examined, the status of the German peasant is worse than it was when Feiler wrote. Agricultural prices, to be sure, have materially improved, but there is a direct correlation between the prices of products which have increased and the type of output of the large estates. Most of the peasant holdings being on a subsistence level, they could not gain much from price advance in any event, and, of course, higher prices for the goods they buy increases their costs of living. The effect upon the rural proletariat has been even more disastrous. Fundamentally, the same picture holds for these two classes in Italy; if anything, the situation is even worse in Italy than in Germany (as is shown in a series of recent articles by a former graduate student of the University of California, and now a member of the Columbia University faculty, Dr. Carl Schmidt).

All this serves to make clear that while the drive of Fascists has been directed toward crushing the threat of mass revolt, they have done nothing to allay the conditions which generated the unrest; rather the reverse. Nor, as indicated by numerous statements of official spokesmen, do they consider it either necessary or important that effort be directed along this line. In fact, the programs articulated not only do not provide for such a change, but involve, on the contrary, an attempt to adjust these sections of their populations in perpetuity to existent conditions, or to any other set of conditions lower or higher that meet with the pleasure of the dominant groups.

In order to effect this end, Fascists have devised the so-called "corporate" state, or system of determinate social categories. These estates, or corporations, or categories—we need not go into a discussion of details of terminology and organization—are set up so as to include, respectively, all members of each occupation within the entire country. Much as in the medieval guilds, and more clearly as in various types of caste systems, each member is supposed to belong to the occupational category into which he was born, and which represents in itself the closest presumptive glove-fit to inherited aptitudes. Thus the carpenter is "born to his calling"—they use this expression in both Italy and Germany—and practices his "nature-determined" occupation throughout life. So likewise with teacher, preacher, journalist, the butcher, the baker, the candlestick maker. The product of success in these regards means fixity of occupation and of social-economic status.

To this is added an elaborate system of regulations to prevent internal migration from carrying with it any tendency toward occupational change. In Germany, for example, the Nazis have passed a national law of entail. Designed, first, to put a stop to the "flight from the land" brought about by the steady degradation of living conditions of the peasants and rural workers, it has been extended so as to make impossible alienation of the land to other than descendants except with the express permission of a representative of the National Food Estate. The peasant cannot sell, cannot endebt, cannot decide not to farm, cannot leave or abandon his farm, cannot leave his district to seek work elsewhere, cannot send his children away, cannot refuse food and asylum to any of first (and in some conditions second) of kin, cannot sell his produce, cannot quote his prices, without express permission. And the permission is typically not granted except under most extenuating circumstances.

Much the same holds for labor in general. All workers carry cards giving an elaborate record of employment, and typically these cannot be honored in a district away from home except under special dispensation. The same holds for certain classes of white-collar workers, and for all classifications of personal and household help. A servant girl from Potsdam, for example, cannot obtain work in Berlin. If she originally came from a Prussian village, she must return there upon termination of her employment in Potsdam. The whole Nazi scheme for small settlement holdings, associated with plans for industrial decentralization, would reduce internal migration to a fraction of its present proportions and make change of residence for labor and the peasantry virtually impossible. Finally, of course, nobody can leave the country at any time nor for any duration of time unless all details are minutely controlled from above. Almost all migrations in and out of the country, except bona fide tourist movements, have been eliminated. In short, under Fascism fixity of residence is on the cards.

All employment in all categories is arranged on the "leader" and "authority" principles. The two combine to give the type of relationship native to the military services: appointment, tenure, and authority from the top down; duty, responsibility, obedience from the bottom up. The employer is the "leader" with full and final "authority" over employees, except as limited by the terms of the industrial code after the pattern provided in the army by the military manuals. That this is the direct inverse of all democratic traditions, outlook, and machinery is obvious on the face of it. But the Fascist governments do not allow the matter to rest there; control extends, also, over the entirety or totality of the life cycle of each subordinate. This is the so-called "total" principle, and means, in effect, that no aspect of life, no feature of thinking, feeling, or believing, no work activity and no leisure-time diversion is left uncoördinated.

These three principles are merely the Fascist way of expressing plans for the *militarization of all social, economic, political, and cultural relationships.* And in this militarization is found, jointly, the means for annihilating all opposition, controlling all thought processes, and keeping in touch— through an elaborate spy system associated therewith—with all movements local or national. The openly confessed object is the *regimented mind,* completely subservient to superior opinion and command, and the conduct of all affairs after the pattern of court-martial proceedings. The atmosphere is that of martial law. This carries over into all civil affairs, almost the entirety of civil and criminal court procedure, for example, being conducted in a military fashion. Trial by jury has been virtually abolished, the accused can be denied legal counsel at will, officials administering the third degree cannot in practice be prosecuted, and the accuser need not be called to substantiate his story before the accused, nor need the accused even be heard. In discussing the law governing the German National Chamber of Culture, the official commentary actually states, *"It is inadmissible that the 'accused' be heard.* The universally valid rule of legal obedience dare not be infringed."*

This entire program has some extremely interesting historical analogies. One thinks immediately of Sparta, certain features of Plato's *Republic* and Aristotle's *Politics,* the Society of Jesus, and the prewar Junker military state. An elaborate supporting doctrine has been worked out in defense of Fascist institutions that is strongly reminiscent in certain elements and moods of these various systems of regimentation.

It will be recalled that Plato assumes in his *Republic* something of the order of a one-to-one correspondence between social station and aptitudes. His analogy of the metals was doubtless borrowed from observations on Sparta, and has in effect been taken over entirely by Fascist theorists. In both Plato and Aristotle the only type of equality which has any meaning is that which gives equal treatment to each individual within his unequal bracket. Thus the "Hellenes" were to rule over the "barbarians," men over women, and the aris-

---

* Italics mine.—R. A. B.

tocracy of what Marshall called "wealth and talents" over those of lower social station. Plato makes specific provision for "sports," that is, for children who are compounded of baser elements but who carry promise of a synthesis towards higher types. Similar provision is made in the systems of both Italy and Germany. In Italy, much is made of Pareto's redaction of the ancient theory in the concept of the "circulating élite." A similar idea is found in the Nazi graduate "leader schools," or seminaries, of which there are now several in various sections of Germany.

The analogy to the system of Plato includes the further idea of the "totalitarian state." For all classes in the *Republic* there was to be, in addition to an appropriate activity, an appropriate propaganda, including all social and cultural activities—music, poetry, literature, the drama, gymnastics, and so forth. And in each the object was (1) to train each individual to do best that for which he was best fitted by nature, and (2) to keep his mind tempered to the point where he desired to be nothing else but what he was. In the sardonic terms of Aldous Huxley's *Brave New World,* each Alpha would choose to be only an Alpha; the Betas would never want to be anything but Betas; the Gammas and Deltas would find nothing else besides what they were doing worth doing at all.

But the analogy ceases here, and shifts to the system of the Jesuits. Loyola added to his "leader," "authority," and "total" principles the concept of complete and final subjection of ideas, and fanatical obedience in all things. In this connection, it is extremely interesting to note that Hitler was brought up a strict Austrian Catholic, and that Goebbels was trained in a Jesuit school before going to Heidelberg. It is no accident, therefore, that Goebbels was quoted as saying, "Anyone may grumble or criticize the government who is not afraid to go to a concentration camp." Under Torquemada anyone could grumble or criticize who was not afraid to go before the Inquisition. And, borrowing from this earlier system, the official commentary on the German Culture Law states: "The sharp, unbridgeable, and absolute opposition of National Socialism to Liberalism lies in the fact that it sets against the idea of a constitutionally guaranteed freedom of ideas, and a state without ideas itself, the notion of an *all-inclusive and decreed idea subjection and idea fixity*."*

Mussolini has achieved the same formula of fanaticism in Italy. The "totalitarian" state of Austria, under the devout Catholic, Schussnigg, follows essentially the same program. In the latter country the borrowing is even more obvious, and papal encyclicals almost automatically acquire the force of law. A particularly noteworthy example of this is to be found in the Austrian semitheocratic organization of occupational categories.

As with the crusading era of the Jesuits, this Fascist program for uniting blind fanaticism and the military pattern turns its attention to the schools and the youth. Mussolini has proudly stated, on numerous occasions, that Fascism is to become "a religion" of hard work, sacrifice, discipline, obedience, and death. War is to be glorified as an end in itself, and to do this it is necessary to begin with the children almost

---

* Italics mine.—R. A. B.

before they leave the cradle. Italian children enter the Children of the She-wolf corps at the age of six, and within a year they have learned the entirety of ordinary military formula and the handling of arms.

The Nazis begin before even this tender age. Hitler has laid down, in *Mein Kampf,* the basic dictum: "Everything, from the baby's first storybook to the last newspaper, theater, cinema ... will be put to this end ... until the brain of the tiniest child is penetrated by the glowing prayer: Almighty God, bless our weapons again ... bless our battle!" And Ley, Leader of the Labor Front, shows how this pattern is followed down through the cycle of the years. "We begin," he says, "with the child of three. As soon as he begins to think we press a little flag into his hand; then comes school, Hitler Youth, the Storm Troops, military service. We do not leave him alone for one moment, and when all that is over, the Labor Front comes and takes possession of him again and does not let him go until death, whether he likes it or not."

Nowhere else can a clearer statement than this be found of the function which militarization of the mind is to perform—to fix the pattern and rivet the controls of the military over the mind in youth as apprenticeship for the pattern all must follow as workmen to the end of their days, whether they like it or not. And thus the military program serves to bring to focus the entire essence of the Fascist system. It provides national support for an enormous industry in armaments and the accouterments of war. Thereby it supplies a market for the products of the heavy industries and a fillip for many of the lighter industries. The resources required come largely out of the lower and middle income brackets, but simultaneously the program "creates" a large amount of employment.

To keep labor employed at low standards, the peasants impoverished, and the middle classes on the narrow edge, is not good business unless a system can be so organized that its principal end products can be disposed of. This the armaments program can do as well as, if not better than, the ordinary type of public works program. Gains can then be funneled back through the economic system, and can be funneled back under circumstances where mass protest can be smothered, and the youth identified with the machine which implements the smothering tactic.

But the condition for this latter is steady promotion of the martial atmosphere and ever-increasing emphasis upon menace to the fatherland, rapacious foes, the duties to civilize barbarian peoples, and other accepted planks in the superpatriotic program. Fascism, says Mussolini, is imperial. It "sees in the imperialistic spirit—i.e. in the tendency of nations to expand—a manifestation of their vitality. In the opposite tendency, which would limit their interests to the fatherland, it sees a symptom of decadence."

War, then, seemingly becomes an end in itself. A German military handbook enthuses over war as a great purifier of the human race. "War," wrote Mussolini, "is the highest expression of Human Genius; war alone keys up all human energies to their maximum tension and sets the seal of nobility to self-sacrifice." And a celebrated Italian futurist, F. T. Marinetti, published, while he was a member of the Italian expeditionary forces in Ethiopa, a manifesto called "Futurist

Aesthetics of War" which caps the climax. As summarized in the *Manchester Guardian:* "War," Marinetti finds, "has a beauty of its own, (1) Because it fuses together in harmony, strength and kindness. Strength alone tends to cruelty and kindness to debility, but the two together 'generate solidarity and generosity.' (2) Because it assures the supremacy of mechanized man—equipped with gas masks, megaphones, flame-throwers and tanks—over his machines. (3) Because it begins the long-dreamed-of metalization of man. (4) Because it completes the beauty of a flowery meadow with its machine guns, "passionate orchids." (5) Because when the symphony of rifle fire and artillery bombardment stops, the songs of soldiers can be heard and the perfumes and odours of putrefaction can be perceived." (There are six more articles yet.)

This is a doctrine that "man is a beast of prey," and it battens on the view that all surviving cultures and civilizations triumph through selection by ordeal of brute strength. It germinates from out a philosophy which has no truck with ideas of humanitarianism or freedom. Its panoply of saints paint its picture and trace its moral code: Nietzsche and his "blond beast" mysticism; von Treitschke and his glorification of the goose-stepping Prussian legionnaire; Houston Stewart Chamberlain, with his scientifically fantastic racial doctrines; Sorel, with his curiously paradoxical doctrines of violence and pretended social myths; Pareto, with his parade of vast learning on behalf of an utterly jejune and scientifically worthless analysis of truncated human behavior patterns; Caesar, the prototype of every hyperthyroid adventurer with the ambition of being the "man on horseback" to his age.

The ethics of these doctrines is frankly amoral. Hence, the heady wine distilled from the grapes of Fascism's Pentateuchal codes may be drunk to the health of flyers returned from annihilation of a Guernica in order to test out the efficiency of a new type of bomber, or may provide a sacrament to the memory of "heroes" lost while dropping incendiary bombs on thatched huts of primitive Ethiopians in order that a small boy's ambition to see a real fire begin might at long last be duly gratified. Just as truth does not count in Fascist universities because veracity is an outmoded virtue there, so human life is unimportant because there are left no criteria for appraising its worth.

But all this does not mean that under Fascism war is an end in itself, even though the official literature so implies. War is merely an ever-present possibility as a by-product of a martial pattern fitted over an entire people by a social-economic oligarchy grown to gigantic proportions from out the chrysalis of competitive capitalistic society. In Italy and Germany a juncture of favorable circumstance with the existence of a highly centralized power of closely-knit economic dynasties stimulated a tightening up by Thermidor to the end that the formal power of the state should no longer serve democratic and popular needs. The forces at play in those nations are no different from those to be found in any Western nation where monopoly-tending blocs have achieved a high degree of centralized power to determine economic policy.

On this analysis, many of the popularly accepted explanations of Fascism are partly or entirely wrong. Thus, it is utterly naïve to regard it as (1) a middle-class revolt, since this confuses a following led to applaud with the initiators of policy. Nor is it (2) a social "sport"—something "accidental," new, and unique to Italy and Germany. The same forces as are behind Fascism in those countries are slowly congealing, slowly becoming interest-conscious, and slowly turning "political" in every nation organized on a capitalistic footing. This means that Fascism is not (3) a destruction of capitalism; rather, it is a final term in capitalism's growth processes from small-scale competition to monopoly forms, and, pari passu, a system in command of political apparatus wherein the profit-and-loss conditions of business survival require wholesale shift from company books to employment of the taxing power of the state.

By the same tokens, Fascism cannot be merely termed (4) a set of devices for "turning back the clock" of culture, for this makes the mistake of identifying as intent that which arises as a result from internal gangrene. It is even more superficial to speak of Fascism (5) as compensation for a national inferiority complex, (6) as Freudian hero worship or "father identification" for postwar neurotic nations, or (7) as a psychological "craving for discipline" and order opposed to disorder of many parties, factions, and so on. These latter explanations come from drawing rooms where dilettantes toy with quaint and exotic ideas, and where the once gay spirit of an outmoded Greenwich village hovers disembodied in the anxious air.

Nor is the idea that Fascism (8) is a reaction to the machine age and its material concepts any closer to reality. But the crowning folly of the superficial mind (9) is to identify Fascism with Communism. One need look no further than to note the array of institutions and ideas condemned by the Fascists as Communism to realize that their anathema includes, along with other things, almost the entirety of the works of Samuel Adams, Thomas Paine, Thomas Jefferson, Abraham Lincoln, and President Roosevelt. But for the last skeptic here, there is still the necessity of a review of spirit, philosophy, fact, and structure. The answer to the question put is clear beyond cavil.

Does the summary and partial analysis of Fascism presented above mean that war is inevitable? I believe that it does. Not because any munitions maker, not because any monopoly-oriented capitalism, not because any other faction or interest involved desires war per se. It is possible that some of them do; but it is not necessary to assume this to be so. Fascism means war for two reasons. In the first place, within the closed political systems of the contemporary world, its expansionist and imperialistic programs cannot possibly avoid war de jure or de facto. For reasons which it would take too long to go into here, but which are inherent in its entire schemata,—particularly its colonial and population policies,—Fascism is necessarily expansionist.

And, in the second place, Fascism means war because it makes revolution—violent, sanguinary, vindictive, and far-flung revolution—inevitable. Revolution is war itself, but the issues range more widely than that. To prevent, deflect, or crush revolution, war will sooner or later be unavoidable, whether or not any subsequent historian is ever able, in accounting therefor, to trace an efficient causal nexus or to uncover a corps of willing initiators. Only the one hope remains that uprisings, when they come, will be so swift and general that Fascism will disappear like a puff of smoke.

I think this highly improbable, and for the following four reasons. First, Fascist propaganda is still too cleverly manipulated, and its hold on the youth which knows nothing else at all is being rooted too deeply. Second, no antidemocratic forces in the annals of human history have been more powerfully entrenched than are those which constitute the backbone of Fascism. Third, the legend of injury, degradation, and wrong which history is swiftly piling up against Fascism has volatile elements in it of such tremendous explosive power that it seems almost inconceivable that they will not be released to ignite the world. Finally, the phenomenon, the growth of processes behind it, and the ever-changing but forever deceptive face of Fascism makes it so difficult for most people to comprehend, that sentiment coagulates against its reaction at a pace which seems too painfully slow.

Here, however, lies the only hope that a general conflagration can be avoided. In a swift mobilization of all the forces of freedom and democracy are to be found whatever hopes there may be for early peace in the cycles of the generations that are to follow.

CONSTITUTIONAL GOVERNMENT
AS A MEANS TO PROMOTE PEACE

———

CHARLES G. HAINES
PROFESSOR OF POLITICAL SCIENCE
IN THE UNIVERSITY OF CALIFORNIA

Lecture delivered October 13, 1937

CONSTITUTIONAL GOVERNMENT
AS A MEANS TO PROMOTE PEACE

DURING THE DEBATES in the federal Convention in Philadelphia, Nathaniel Gorham asked whether it could "be
supposed that this vast country including the western territory will one hundred fifty years hence remain one nation."[1]
The most optimistic of the delegates to that Convention could
not have foreseen the extent of the territory and the large
population now under the jurisdiction of the federal Union,
and the important position which the political system they
were about to establish would hold among the nations of the
world. It is appropriate at the end of the first half of the second century since the Constitution for the thirteen states on
the Atlantic seaboard was drafted, to evaluate the advantages
which have ensued from the operation of government under
the charter which was drafted in 1787.[2]

I

Constitutional government, as it was taking form in the
American states during the last decades of the eighteenth century, was based on four primary principles: *first,* that there
is a hierarchy of laws, some being of such a superior character
that they condition all civil and political conduct; *second,*

---

[1] Max Farrand, *Records of the Federal Convention*, II:221.

[2] The scope of the present discussion is limited primarily to the principles
and practices of constitutional government as developed and understood in
the United States. Except for some brief references and comparisons no attempt will be made to consider the significance or the future of constitutional
government in foreign countries.

that the individual has certain inherent personal and individual rights and that these must be protected from all serious hazards; *third,* that there is special virtue in putting the essential and underlying principles for the guidance of political conduct into written form that they may be known and respected,—hence a written constitution is an agency or instrument for individual security and good government; *fourth,* that special precautions and procedure should be taken to assure the enforcement of the limits on governmental powers.

James Madison, defending the document framed in Philadelphia, thought the ends of free government were, first, to protect the people against their rulers, and second, to protect them against the transient impressions into which they themselves might be led. These ends have been substantially attained by the adoption of a federal fundamental law. The Constitution of 1787 not only has served as an effective instrument for the establishment of a central government for the nation, but also has been an appropriate device to protect citizens in the preservation of their individual rights and privileges. Above all it has assured for the governmental system of the United States a basic régime according to law. With a century and a half of our constitutional history in perspective, Anatole France's observation appears especially appropriate—"that popular government, like monarchy, rests on fiction and lives by expedients. It suffices that the fiction be accepted and the expedient happy." It will be my purpose to discuss briefly some of the fictions and expedients which have accompanied the growth of constitutional government, particularly as it has developed in the United States.

It is customary to regard the procedure in the formation of the federal Constitution as an epoch-making event in the evolution of a representative type of government based on popular support. According to James Wilson, one of the foremost members of the Philadelphia Convention, America presented "the first instance of a people assembled to weigh deliberately and calmly, and to decide leisurely and peaceably, upon the form of government by which they will bind themselves and their posterity."[3]

However, instead of the calm, deliberate, and peaceable procedure to which Wilson referred, the Constitution was framed as a result of a revolutionary process in which the instructions to the convention delegates were not followed and the legal requirements for the amendment of the Articles of Confederation were ignored. And in place of the calm and deliberate procedure in the adoption of the plan drafted at Philadelphia, there was, as Elbridge Gerry observed, an inordinate zeal to secure by every possible means an early adoption of the Constitution as drafted.

Historians have been accumulating evidence which makes it apparent that the adoption of the Constitution was accomplished by a coup d'état through which the conservative and aristocratic groups took advantage of a fortunate set of circumstances and by every known political device and maneuver secured adoption before the liberal and radical classes of the people, comprising a majority in most of the states, could satisfactorily organize their forces.

John Adams, a close observer of the constitution-making

---

[3] *New York Daily Advertiser*, December 3, 1787.

process, noted that the federal Convention was the work of the commercial people in the seaport towns, of the planters of the slave-holding states, and of the officers of the Revolutionary Army, and that these groups could not have succeeded in securing the adoption of the Constitution "had they not received the active and steady coöperation of all that was left in America of the attachment to the mother country, as well as the moneyed interest, which ever points to strong government as the needle to the pole."[4] This is a frank recognition of the class basis for the formation and adoption of the Constitution. The men who accomplished the coup d'état no doubt believed that they not only were protecting their own interests but also were taking a step which would inure to the public good.

It is well to remember in the clash of opinion over the interpretation of the Constitution that the document had its origin in differences between the conservative and liberal groups similar to those with which we are familiar today. And in forming a judgment on some of the controversial issues presented to the people relating to the meaning of the fundamental law and its significance in a twentieth-century society the class origin of the document must be considered.

The assertion made by Woodrow Wilson and frequently quoted by others, that contemporaneously with the adoption of the Constitution criticism of its provisions not only ceased but gave place to "an undiscriminating and almost blind worship of its principles,"[5] by no means represents the prevail-

[4] *Works*, I:441–443.
[5] *Congressional Government . . .* (Boston, 1925), p. 4.

ing impressions regarding the Constitution until toward the middle of the nineteenth century. Hamilton in a moment of impatience and disgust prophesied that the worthless fabric could not endure, and there were many more than we are ordinarily led to believe who agreed with Richard Henry Lee, a member of the federal Convention, and the Democratic Senator Maclay from Pennsylvania, that the Constitution was likely to serve as a trap "to ensnare the freedom of an unsuspecting people." For at least twenty-five years the leaders of all parties turned to the states as the normal and natural custodians of public authority. Thinking that the experiment of a federal Union under the Constitution was likely to fail, they were willing to try some other form of political coöperation. It was this sentiment which led to the separatist movement in New England and the calling of the Hartford Convention in 1814 to consider ways and means of secession. But the success of the new government tended to allay the critical attitude of the people during the first few decades.

Economic conditions, no doubt, were largely responsible for the shift in public sentiment which led to the formation of the federal Constitution. The defects of the Articles of Confederation were exaggerated by the difficulties and distress of an industrial depression, and the federal government was organized at a time when the tide of economic and industrial prosperity began to return. It was not long, therefore, before the confidence, contentment, and generally improved conditions which prevailed were attributed to the adoption of the Constitution.

Though the Federalists and Anti-Federalists, or the Democratic-Republicans, as they were beginning to be called, differed over the interpretation of the provisions of the Constitution, they soon joined in extolling the virtues of the written instrument. The work of the framers then wrought in the turmoil and bitterness of party strife and inaugurated, as Washington and Hamilton believed, as "an experiment," became the symbol of a Golden Age. Judge Addison of Pennsylvania, who was impeached by the Democratic legislature of the state for Federalist speeches and conduct from the bench, expressed the sentiment which grew in popularity. Man, he thought, "must have an idol. And our political idol ought to be the Constitution and the laws. They, like the ark of covenant among the Jews, ought to be sacred from all profane touch."[6] The practice was begun at this time for the defeated party to take refuge behind the Constitution and the Supreme Court as its expounder, and to insist on obedience to the letter of the written instrument. The party in power, on the other hand, responsible for the welfare of the people and the constructive action required to preserve that welfare, found it necessary to take a liberal and latitudinarian view of the provisions of the basic law.

Thus the development of constitutional government in the United States as well as in England reflected the struggle for power of the dominant classes of society. It is well known that the adoption of Magna Carta and of other English charters of liberties resulted from the wresting of privileges from the king and other groups of barons and land owners, by certain groups of the nobility. And in England as in the

---

[6] *Addison Reports* (1800), Appendix, p. 242.

United States a kind of halo of popular sanctity was ascribed to the written document because its acceptance was hailed as a guarantee of peace, order, and good government and as a warrant against arbitrary action in public administration. Though there was little support for the belief that written charters were a substantial aid in securing equal and fair privileges to all citizens, aristocratically conceived and promulgated documents were nevertheless from the beginning surrounded by a sort of democratic aroma. Following the English procedure of putting into written form the individual rights and privileges which were deemed most sacred and which were to be secure from unreasonable interference, some of the principles of the Declaration of Independence and of the radical party which conducted affairs during the Revolutionary period were enacted into the first ten amendments to the federal Constitution as a Bill of Rights. Though this step marked a concession to the popular tendencies of the day, it required a series of political revolts such as those led by Jefferson, Jackson, and Lincoln to turn the trend of constitutional interpretation partly in the direction of democratic policies and theories.

II

When the Jeffersonian revolution brought a radical change in the executive and legislative departments, and public sentiment no longer supported the conservative and aristocratic tendencies which had prevailed during the Federalist administrations, the Constitution was conceived as an instrument to carry out democratic purposes. William E. Dodd's contention that the legal arrangements in both the state and the federal constitutions were designed to defeat and thwart democracy[7] may be only partly true, but it is apparent that the makers of written constitutions hoped through these instruments to check the trend toward popular control of government and to safeguard the rights of property and contract. The Massachusetts constitution of 1780, largely the handiwork of John Adams, as Samuel E. Morison notes, was "a lawyer's and merchant's constitution, directed toward something like quarterdeck efficiency in government and the protection of property against democratic pirates." In a similar manner, though aiming to establish a reasonably strong government, the members of the Philadelphia Convention were determined to check the rising tide of democracy. The Democratic-Republican party, however, found that it could adapt the Constitution to the aims and purposes of the party and had it not been for the Supreme Court and its spokesman, Chief Justice Marshall, the federal Constitution might have become the vehicle to lead the nation, subject to few legal obstructions, in the direction of democratic ideals and practices.

In *Marbury v. Madison,*[8] Marshall, as Albert J. Beveridge points out, prepared his answer to the Democratic and States Rights version of interpreting the provisions of the Constitution. The Supreme Court was henceforth to be the ultimate interpreter of the Constitution, and the executive and legislative departments were to be subject to its surveillance. In *Fletcher v. Peck*[9] and *Dartmouth College v. Woodward,*[10] cor-

---

[7] Cf. "The Struggle for Democracy in the United States," *International Journal of Ethics*, XXVIII:465 (July, 1918).

[8] 1 Cranch 137 (1903).   [9] 6 Cranch 87 (1810).   [10] 4 Wheat. 518 (1819).

porations were brought within the scope of the protection of the contract clause of the Constitution and the artificial bodies created by the states were given a superior position which could readily be translated into industrial dominance over the agencies of civic control and management. These decisions, Justice Story thought, would check encroachments upon civil rights, which the passions and popular doctrines of the people might stimulate state legislatures to adopt, and Sir Henry Maine lauded them as "the bulwark of American individualism against Democratic impatience and Socialistic fantasy."[11] And in a series of masterly decisions the great Federalist Chief Justice sustained the supremacy of the federal government and humiliated the states claiming sovereign rights and privileges. Thus three of the leading aims and objectives of the Federalist party—judicial review of the validity of acts of Congress, protection from governmental interference with the vested rights of property and with contracts for corporations as well as for individuals, and the expansion of the powers of the federal government through a doctrine of implied or resulting powers—were by judicial interpretation made an integral part of federal constitutional law.

Though the majority of the members of the Supreme Court were affiliated with the Democratic-Republican party, they joined with the Chief Justice in supporting the Federalistic and nationalistic theories of constitutional interpretation. And the leaders of the Democratic faith and philosophy found an effective barrier in decisions of the Supreme Court to the carrying out of some of their primary objectives. When

[11] See Albert J. Beveridge, *The Life of John Marshall*, IV:277 ff.

the Supreme Court placed its position and authority in support of the nationalistic trends of the time and in defense of incipient commercial and industrial undertakings the Court came to be regarded as the structure on which the real support of the Constitution rested. Daniel Webster argued that without exercise by the Supreme Court of the powers which the Federalists insisted belonged to the Court, there would be no Constitution.

The Jacksonian Democrats checked for the time being the nationalistic leanings of the justices. And under the Chief Justiceship of Roger B. Taney an attempt was made to direct the trend of constitutional interpretation to a greater degree toward the protection of public rather than private interests, and to restore to the states some of the rights which they said were taken from them by judicial construction. But the main course of the stream of constitutional construction was not diverted from its former channel. The Court gradually came under the control of the slave owners and rendered the Dred Scott decision which aided in precipitating the Civil War and in subordinating the Constitution and the Court to the political forces of the country for nearly two decades.

Following the Civil War, new economic and industrial leaders took over the management of the country and their influence was soon felt in the decisions of the Supreme Court. The constitutional amendments enacted to protect human rights and to grant equal privileges to the Negro were held to apply to corporations, and the wielders of economic power quickly took advantage of the situation. Due process of law, equal protection of the laws, the judicially construed doctrine of liberty of contract, as well as other constitutional phrases, were the constitutional pegs on which to fasten a new type of conservatism, and to defeat the attempt to enact measures designed to regulate social and industrial affairs. The appeals to the federal courts by corporate organizations and the holders of the fluid wealth of the country were legion. On the other hand, the appeals to secure protection for individual rights were few and seldom successful. The Supreme Court, as in the times of Marshall and Taney, threw its weight in favor of the economically strong and powerful. While the government was being importuned to grant all kinds of advantages and favors to special interests the courts were developing a laissez-faire policy which gave industrial leaders the freedom from political meddling which they desired. The Supreme Court justices who feared the trend toward social control of business, as Justice Holmes repeatedly asserted, were subconsciously and unintentionally, perhaps, reading their economic and political predilections into the Constitution and then using the newly construed phrases to strike down economic and social legislation. Constitutional government as it developed in the United States before and after the World War, not so much through changes in the fundamental law as through the method of judicial construction, was becoming to a greater degree than at any time in our history what the Federalists had designed that it should be— an agency to foster the interests of special groups or classes.

And again the Supreme Court is being lauded as not only the central feature of the Constitution but also as the agency without which there would be no Constitution. According to

Nicholas Murray Butler, the Supreme Court "is the only representative which the American people have to which they may turn for the protection of the underlying principles of their government" and this department, in his judgment, must not be deprived of its power "to interpret the fundamental principles of government itself."[12] Similar to the analysis of John Adams, Butler's conception of the Constitution and the Court is that they are the primary means of protecting the interests of particular groups. The representatives elected by the people, and the executive given a mandate to carry out their wishes, do not know what are the fundamental principles of the government. No other individuals or groups of individuals know what these principles are. This is indeed equivalent to the assertion that the Constitution is not made for the people and to serve the people, but the people live for and are servants of the Constitution. Constitutional law is not a way and means for securing the life, liberty, and happiness of all the people. Apparently the only things fundamental to American citizens are the protection of the private and property rights which the Supreme Court has vouchsafed.

Thus the device of a written constitution became the medium through which conservative policies were to be discovered and applied by the process of judicial construction. This result was accomplished to a considerable degree because the courts, as Justice Stone has pointed out, applied to questions of constitutional power a common-law technique. The continuous practice of searching the past and following precedents not only stamped constitutional law with a certain type

---

[12] *New York Times*, April 19, 1937.

of conservatism, but also led to the placing of shackles on political action because of the habit of mind with which lawyers and judges approach a decision when no precedent necessarily controls. Mechanical appraisals often resulted which were characterized by sterile formalism. Following the common-law technique and the professed application of the doctrine of *stare decisis,* judges narrowed the judicial lawmaking function which has been the most important feature of the common law and failed to relate constitutional decisions, as Stone observes, to "the social data to which the law must be attuned if it is to fulfill its purpose."[13]

Constitutional law, however, need not be "an aggregate of hard and fast precepts to be handed on and followed from generation to generation." The principles and maxims of the fundamental law may serve as starting points for legal reasoning and legal technique in developing the ideal of a reasonable exercise of the powers of politically organized society. From this standpoint, the Constitution forms the groundwork for a continuity not of rules but of aims and ideals, and its language may be adapted to what Justice Holmes called "preponderant public opinion."

It is largely because a written Constitution amended in only a few important respects since the early nineteenth century has not been interpreted in a too literal or mechanical manner that it has continued to serve adequately the needs of a large and growing nation. In the first place, the assertion that the meaning of the Constitution does not change, that what it

---

[13] Justice Harlan F. Stone, "The Common Law in the United States," 50 *Harv. Law Rev.* (November, 1936), p. 6.

meant when it came from the hands of the framers it means now, though given utterance on various occasions, has not been the dominant view in constitutional interpretation. On the other hand, as Justice Brandeis maintains, the Constitution must have a capacity of adaptation to a changing world, and in the application of the Constitution "our contemplation cannot be only of what has been but of what may be. Under any other rule a constitution would indeed be as easy of application as it would be deficient in efficacy and power. Its general principles would have little value and be converted by precedent into impotent and lifeless formulas."[14]

In the second place, the Constitution has not proved to be too serious a barrier or obstruction when conditions required the use of emergency powers. Beginning with the Force Bill authorizing President Washington to quell the Whiskey Insurrection in Pennsylvania, presidents have been granted something approaching dictatorial powers in every war or minor conflict in which the nation has been engaged. When the query was put to Jefferson, after his purchase of Louisiana and the unsuccessful effort to secure an amendment to authorize the purchase and sanction the administration of the territory, how he justified his conduct, he replied that he did so on the emergency-power doctrine. "A strict observance of the written laws," he thought, "is doubtless one of the high duties of a good citizen, but it is not the highest. The laws of necessity, of self-preservation, of saving our country when in danger, are of higher obligation."[15] Thus Presidents Lincoln,

---

[14] Justice Brandeis, dissenting in *Olmsted v. United States,* 277 U. S. 438, 473 (1927).

[15] *Works* (Ford ed.), IX:279, 280.

Wilson, and Franklin D. Roosevelt exercised with and without the approval of Congress emergency powers designed to
save the country and to preserve the welfare of the people.
And the crisis which we face today in the consideration of
proposed judicial reforms comes largely from the prevailing
practice of making the written document a lawyer's document which, not by express language but by judicial construction, has become an effective means of preventing the carrying
out of the public policies approved by the people.

III

The most significant feature of a written constitution such as
that prepared in Philadelphia, however, is not to be found
in the language and provisions of the instrument itself nor in
the interpretation of its words and phrases by those responsible for its application at any particular time, but in the use
of the instrument for the development of legal fictions and
myths. Alexander Hamilton, who had little respect for popular government, formulated one of the basic fictions of American constitutional law. Defending the doctrine that with a
written constitution defining and limiting the powers of
government it was the duty and function of the judiciary to
be the guardian and ultimate interpreter of the document,
Hamilton contended that such a procedure was necessary to
establish the rule of the people. A body of judges, appointed
for life, independent of all governmental agencies, declaring
the meaning of the written instrument—this was the Hamiltonian version of the rule of the people. It is not difficult to
understand why Hamilton wanted to have judges as the final

interpreters of the fundamental law, for he not only distrusted the people but he would also have reduced their participation in public affairs to a minimum. It is not so readily apparent why those who profess to believe in the principles and practices of popular government have continued to repeat and to approve this basic myth.

Judges who began to assert their supremacy over the other departments of government so far as the interpretation of the Constitution is concerned, and those who thought the courts by this means could maintain an effective check upon the vagaries of popular majorities, joined in asserting that the courts in exercising the authority of judicial review do not veto legislation. Prominent members of the bar have insisted that justices never have thought of such a thing as a veto. Here is another fiction which the written constitution has fostered. A law is passed by both houses of the legislature and signed by the executive. By all the rules and canons of legislation it is a law from the date when it is declared to take effect. All citizens affected by the law must obey the act. But an individual adversely affected by the act brings a case to the courts. The judges deem the act invalid; and a sit-down strike results, for the law cannot be enforced. So far as the litigants in the case and all other citizens affected by the law are concerned, the act is no longer applicable and effective. The act, it is insisted, has not been vetoed, it is merely void, invalid, and of no effect. To maintain the fiction, however, it must not be called a veto.

With the assumption in which there was general agreement that a written constitution is a superior or fundamental law and that legislative and executive acts performed under its provisions are subordinate and inferior laws, it was assumed to be the duty of the judges to place the legislative or executive act side by side with the Constitution, and if there appeared, as they understood the requirements of the written language, an irreconcilable conflict, the will of the people had to be sustained rather than the acts of public officers. There are few decisions, however, on constitutional issues affecting the vital interests of the people in which the laying of Constitution and statute side by side leads to any indubitable conclusion. The conflict, if there is any, when the words of the Constitution are vague or do not give a direct mandate to the Court, depends upon the interpretation of language and in such interpretation the training, interests, point of view, and philosophy of the justices play a prominent part. In this field, which now comprises the major part of the most important constitutional controversies, the judges actively participate in the legislative process. But the fiction still persists that the justices act only in a mechanical and impartial manner in applying the terms and provisions of the written fundamental law, and that their personal, political, and social views and predilections have no bearing whatever on their judgments and opinions.

The most persistent and the most generally accepted fiction relating to the Supreme Court's interpretation of the provisions of the Constitution is that the Court in guarding the Constitution has been a bulwark for the protection of civil and religious liberties. Numerous studies have been made which have called attention to the relatively few occasions on which the Supreme Court has given substantial protection to individuals whose civil or religious liberties have been violated. In a recent analysis of the cases in which the Supreme Court declared acts of Congress void, Professor Henderson of Cornell University concludes that "there is not a case in the entire series which protected civil liberties of freedom of speech, press, and assembly; on the contrary, over the protest of Holmes and Brandeis, the Espionage Act was not merely upheld but extended by the Court. There is not one which protected the right to vote; on the contrary, congressional attempts to protect the voting rights of Negroes were defeated by the Court. There is not one which protected the vital interests of the working majority of the population in organizing or in wages; on the contrary, congressional efforts to protect those interests were frustrated by the Court." The cases usually cited give, as Mr. Henderson demonstrates, small support to the theory that Congress has attacked and judicial supremacy defended the citizen's liberty.[16] It is surprising in view of the customary declamations and oratorical flourishes along this line to examine the record and note how many more cases there are wherein the courts protected the government against the citizen, gave their sanction to unfair and unreasonable business activities, deprived Negroes of rights which were presumed to be guaranteed, defended business interests in preference to the cause of the laboring man, and gave privileges and preferences to the large owners of property and taxpayers. The protection accorded to indi-

[16] Henry W. Edgerton, "The Incidence of Judicial Control over Congress," 22 *Cornell Law. Quar.* (April, 1937), pp. 299 ff.

viduals against the arbitrary acts of the states in trials under the criminal syndicalism acts and in the trial of Negroes has been widely publicized as indicative of the decisions to be expected from the Justices in similar cases. But these decisions have merely tended to camouflage the fact that the prevailing decisions of the Court in reviewing and declaring void acts of Congress have tended to favor the interests of the rich and well-to-do rather than to preserve and protect the rights and liberties of the common man.

The discussion of the place and function of the courts in our federal system is saturated with fictions and myths that have a meager foundation in fact. Attention has recently been directed to the fictional and symbolic features of much that passes current as the essence of American constitutionalism.[17] To expose legal myths or fictions apparently has little effect upon the popular impressions which have gained currency through propaganda and misrepresentation, for stubborn theories are often much more persistent and more domineering than stubborn facts. Moreover, in some respects the adoration of the Constitution as an idol has exceeded the hopes and wishes of Judge Addison and others who looked forward to the worship of the written fundamental law.

Though constitutionalism in the United States with its characteristic fictions and myths has at times dulled the moral and political responsibility of the people and to a certain extent has made the processes of government covert and com-

---

[17] See Edward S. Corwin, "The Constitution as Instrument and Symbol," 30 *Amer. Pol. Science Rev.* (December, 1936), p. 1071, and Max Lerner, "Constitution and Court as Symbols," 46 *Yale Law Jour.* (June, 1937), p. 1290.

plicated with the opportunity for special interests to secure
their ends through indirect channels, the interpretation and
application of the written fundamental law has at other times
aided in accomplishing the objectives of the liberal and democratic parties. In the main, the attainment of peace, order, and
good government of a nonarbitrary type has been accomplished to a substantial degree for all citizens. Each time that
constitutional interpretation has turned in the direction of
the protection of special privileges, political leaders as well as
jurists have joined to change the trend toward the democratic
approach and outlook. I do not know much about law, said
Theodore Roosevelt, but I do know one can put the fear of
God into judges. His campaign for the recall of judicial decisions changed the course of the interpretation of constitutional provisions in a liberal direction for nearly two decades.
And one may surmise whether it was the fear of God or the
fear of the loss of prestige and power which impelled the odd
man to change his vote on minimum-wage laws, thereby ren-
dering them constitutional, after Franklin D. Roosevelt proposed a change in the Supreme Court personnel.

IV

The makers of constitutions in the late eighteenth and early
nineteenth centuries attached a significance to the provisions
of written fundamental laws which does not accord with
some of the foremost tendencies of modern political life. It
was thought that the underlying principles of government
were relatively simple, and that once they were discovered it
was necessary to express them in permanent written form.

Not only were rulers and ruled to be guided by the terms and conditions thus enshrined, but also the mere formulation of essential norms and principles of political conduct was regarded as a guarantee of good government. Constitutionalism, which has been characterized as "the trust which men repose in the power of words engrossed on parchment to keep a government in order," had its effective beginnings in America, where it had its formal christening with the enactment of the constitutions for the states in 1776. The instrument framed in Philadelphia and put into effect in 1789 made these principles an integral part of American national life. The spread of constitutionalism, which was one of the foremost characteristics of the nineteenth century, was molded largely in accordance with American ideals and concepts.

So important and essential were deemed the purposes and objects of written constitutions that during the nineteenth century most countries, as they developed democratic and representative institutions, adopted written constitutions. The movement after a temporary lull emerged into a special wave of constitution making after the World War. But the tide of political idealism at this time was followed by a reaction which has led to the repudiation of constitutional government in so many states that the high hopes of those who looked forward to a time when the people in all but a few nations would be living under a parliamentary and constitutional régime were rudely shattered.

But are forms of government the most important factor in the establishment and maintenance of national or world peace? Do not social, economic, and industrial factors condition and determine the essential policies of nations, rather than political notions? The way by which elaborate and detailed provisions inserted in written charters have been ignored by the various factions in control of public affairs in Latin-American countries is notorious. Governments, whether monarchic, oligarchic, democratic, or dictatorial may pursue unreasonable, arbitrary, and tyrannical methods backed by military force to gain their ends. Our own record in the extension of our domains bears witness to the fact that nations under parliamentary institutions may resort to military action at the expense of weaker countries on flimsy pretexts. More depends upon the traditions, attitude, and spirit of the people, in the determination of whether governmental policies shall be controlled by the will and caprice of small groups of individuals or shall be under a régime of law with popular sanction or approval.

Although no nation has been continuously under the guidance of principles of justice or the rule of law, it is nevertheless apparent that a written constitution, which has been characterized as the rules of the game designed to assure fair play, has a tendency to limit arbitrary action and to check the resort to violence in gaining political and economic ends. And although the decline in the attachment to and the sentiment for written constitutions according to nineteenth-century standards is unmistakable and constitutes one of the most significant trends in modern political practice, it does not appear probable that written constitutions have outlived their usefulness. By such instruments, maintains Justice Cardozo, "the great ideals of liberty and equality have often been preserved against the assaults of opportunism, the expediency of the passing hours, the erosion of small encroachments, the scorn and derision of those who have no patience with general principles."[18] The chief worth of a written instrument no doubt lies in making clear and readily defensible the ideals and principles that might otherwise be ignored and in giving them continuity of life and expression.

And the federal Constitution drafted in 1787 has not only accomplished this object but it has also served to maintain, as a rule, a delicate balance between order and liberty. Many believe that the one great issue that overshadows all others in the world today is the issue between constitutionalism and arbitrary government, and whether constitutionalism can survive under modern social and economic conditions. Differences between monarchy and democracy, or between capitalism, socialism, and communism, are regarded as minor in comparison with the conflict between representative and democratic or dictatorial forms of government. "Deeper than the problem whether we shall have a capitalistic system or some other enshrined in our law," thinks Professor McIlwain, "lies the question whether we shall be ruled by law at all, or only by arbitrary will."[19]

Observers of international affairs regretfully admit that the liberal democracies of the world are retreating before the forces of violence and aggression. In opposition to these alarming and devastating policies of arbitrary action, terror-

---

[18] Benjamin N. Cardozo, *The Nature of the Judicial Process* (New Haven, 1921), pp. 92–94.

[19] C. H. McIlwain, "Government by Law," 14 *Foreign Affairs* (January, 1936), p. 185.

ism, and aggressive warfare, which are obliterating the ideals of liberalism and democracy prevalent during the nineteenth century and the postwar period, the liberal governments of today appear to be losing ground. With the continuance and extension of dictatorships in Europe, Asia, and Latin America and the precarious situation of parliamentary institutions in France, only England with her Self-Governing Colonies and the United States remain among the leading nations of the world in which representative governments of the parliamentary type with the democratic procedure characteristic of such a system are still in successful operation.

And though we may scan the century and a half since the formation of our federal Constitution with a feeling of profound satisfaction that our forefathers wrought wisely and with unusual foresight when they prepared a frame of government for a union of the separate and independent states of the Revolutionary period, it is true nevertheless that the leaders of today face a grave responsibility of devising ways and means to adapt the instrument the substantial provisions of which were drafted in the eighteenth century, to the conditions and requirements of the twentieth century.

American constitutional law has been to a considerable degree the result of political action accomplished through judicial methods. The process has been sustained and sanctioned largely by the persistence of the fiction that only legal logic and the literal application of the language of the Constitution have been involved. No doubt the belief in this fiction served a useful purpose in the formative years of constitutional development, but today it is fostered chiefly by the uninitiated in the field of constitutional interpretation, or by those who find it to their advantage to encourage reverence for outworn traditions and doctrines. It is strange that there should be so much concern at the present time that the federal Constitution has been treated as a political document and as involving more than legal mechanics in the application of its provisions from the time of its formation. As a general practice, when occasions seemed to require, the people as well as Congress and the President have not hesitated to treat the Constitution and the courts as agencies of effectuating the nation's policies and of controlling them so far as necessary to accomplish these ends.

Despite the prevailing tradition and the popular belief based thereupon that the Constitution of the United States is law in the customary sense of that term, is it not time to discard the fiction and pretense that the judges in interpreting the Constitution are merely expounding the will of the makers and are applying the exact and invariable legal meaning of the terms and phrases of the written document?

The records of history tend to show unmistakably that for constitutional government to endure it is necessary that it be based on a living law rather than a law encased in judicial precedents and bound by mechanical formulas presumed to emanate from a written instrument. And a survey of the American constitutional development since 1789 demonstrates the advisability and necessity that the fundamental law embody in more than a fictional and mythical sense the real will and purposes of the nation. For, as Abraham Lincoln contended in his debates with Stephen A. Douglas, "the people are the rightful masters of both Congress and the Courts—not to overthrow the Constitution but to overthrow the men who pervert it. Legislation and adjudication must follow and conform to the progress of society."

THE PROBLEM OF
WORLD ORGANIZATION

MALBONE W. GRAHAM

PROFESSOR OF POLITICAL SCIENCE
IN THE UNIVERSITY OF CALIFORNIA

Lecture delivered October 20, 1937

THE PROBLEM OF
WORLD ORGANIZATION

DURING THIS sesquicentennial year, commemorative of our national Constitution, there has been frequent occasion to stop and take stock of our institutional heritage in the constitutional field, attempting to appraise, after an interval of a century and a half, the functioning and worth of the agencies established by that instrument. The task has been one of unusual interest; the possibility of determining what was the permanent and what the impermanent in the work of the Founding Fathers has been vouchsafed to our day and age, if only by the sheer fact of the lapse of time. The abiding values have been made evident, as also the means chosen by the men of that generation to remedy the palpable defects of the social and legal order in the then very loosely associated States. And yet I have not been able to dissociate my attitude toward them and their task from that which I have toward the one which lies before us in the present discussion—the integral problem of international organization, viewed in the retrospect of only twenty years. And just as our own Founding Fathers held inquest, rather than inquiry, over the loose League of Amity and Friendship which had been founded but a brief decade before, under the Articles of Confederation, and my initial task is not wholly dissimilar, my readers will, I hope, forgive any disappointment which parts of my analysis may reveal. If it exists, it is inherent in the historical facts; the potentialities of international organization are still dynamic.

Few will deny that the status of international organization at the present time is as unsatisfactory and precarious as that of our own Union toward the close of the "critical period" a little over one hundred and fifty years ago, not so much on its institutional side as in its actual functioning and jurisdictional limitations. In both, we have to deal with a performance under a written charter of authority falling far short of legitimate anticipations; in both there were wanting the stuff and substance of an affirmative jurisdiction, directly operative upon the component states. It is apparent to the most casual observer of the present ensemble of institutions performing the functions of world government that, like our own at the confederal stage, their fiscal resources are extremely small, that they possess no direct revenues enabling them to develop an autonomous momentum, that they exercise practically no coercive power upon members, and that no independent force lies at their disposal for procuring compliance with their decisions. In short, save for the existence of agencies capable of expeditious settlement of litigious questions the political institutions of international government are to be placed—with a time lag of approximately one hundred and thirty years—exactly where the thirteen ex-colonies found themselves at the end of a decade of slowly dissolving confederal government. We stand in a new "critical period," this time in relation to world, rather than national, organization.

Now the men who foregathered in Philadelphia a century and a half ago had a lawful mandate to amend, even as existing agencies, at Geneva and elsewhere, are equally empowered to propose paper amendments; but the problem goes far deeper, and digs down to the very fundamentals of government. That is why I purpose to push aside most of the numerous suggestions for amendment of the Genevan Ark of the Covenant, as well as the largely spiritual wish-thinking accompanying the efforts at harmonization of the Covenant and the Kellogg Pact,—a process once compared by a cynical Fascist diplomat to the hybridization of a contract and a prayer,—and go back to the efforts made at the close of the World War to organize the whole scheme of international government and determine whether the fault, if fault there be, does not lie there. Without here attempting to prejudge the findings, I believe we shall find a rather large quarry, filled with stones which the builders rejected. Some of this material may yet prove of value in building the House of Peace.

The quarry contains a varied assortment of ideas contributed during the period of the World War by individuals of low and high estate, by groups with the reformer complex, by pontifically solemn learned societies, and even by governments. They are overlaid with the ideological débris and covered by the water that has gone under the bridge of history in the postwar years. Hence it requires some tenacity of purpose and a distinct methodology to get at them. In the space at my disposal I cannot hope to reëxcavate the entire quarry, but I believe we can recover some of our ideological losses. At all events we must get back to bedrock facts.

May I begin for our purpose with the hectic period of definition of war aims in 1918—the rapid barrage and counter-barrage of ideas which produced the Wilsonian Fourteen Points. These crystallized, out of the heat and the fires of war, certain ideological touchstones destined to be enormously influential in the conclusion of peace. I think it safe to say that none of these was more significant than the fourteenth—the Wilsonian premise of a new world order: *"A general association* of nations *under specific covenants* for the purpose of affording mutual guarantees of political independence and territorial integrity to great and small states alike."

And yet, when one seeks to probe into the recesses of President Wilson's mind, from the evidence given in his public utterances, his conception of the general nature of the association, of the form and content of the mutual guarantees,— other than those of a territorial character,—becomes vague and elusive. Only one thing is clear: the general international organization to be established must be based on specific, and therefore written, covenants.[1] In taking this stand almost at the outset of the ideological battle, Wilson aligned himself with the proponents of a *written* constitution for the new world order, one capable of strict and meticulous construction by legalistic minds. In so doing Wilson revealed himself as

---

[1] Characteristic of the evolution of the President's ideas is the fact that when he enunciated, in the great Metropolitan Opera House address of September 27, 1918, his concretized conceptions of the content of its *covenants,* they were essentially negative: no discrimination between states; no special interests; no leagues or alliances or special covenants within the general family; no special, selfish economic combinations, and no secret diplomacy. Here Wilson, the Virginian, insisted on his negative, limiting, Bill of Rights before stating the positive contents of his credo. By December 16, 1918, he told a French Socialist delegation of his desire for "a coöperation of the nations which shall be based upon *fixed and definite covenants";* at the Guildhall in London a fortnight later he told the Lord Mayor and the British Government: "I am eager to get at the business and *write the sentences down."—The Public Papers of Woodrow Wilson,* V:161, 255, 326, 343. (Italics mine.—M. W. G.)

the perfect inheritor of strictly American conceptions of a government of limited powers. By his stand he was precommitted to a written charter or constitution with all the limitations inherent in it, when applying the methodology of constitutionalism to a field theretofore dominated by power politics.

In vivid contrast with this conception of a crystalloid Covenant was the British idea of an *unwritten constitution, an amorphous and colloid covenant* for the associated nations. Curiously, this, although pervasively held, is one of the hardest conceptions to make clear and buttress, for the paradoxical reason that its very essence consisted in continuous but unwritten understandings, which, if ever recorded to any substantial degree, quite defeated their own ends. Nevertheless, the British approach and technique were alike clear. Building on the traditions and tacit understandings of cabinet government, of imperial conferences, and the like, they intended to make the League of Nations an ensemble of accepted usages and understandings, with as few written commitments as possible, and with no territorial guarantees whatsoever. By imposing on the League a series of general tasks and a number of specific ones,[2] they thought to leave its global jurisdic-

---

[2] A brief enumeration reveals the extent to which it was intended to invest the League with full powers of direct territorial government. At one time or another it was proposed that the League directly or indirectly govern (1) Constantinople and the Straits, (2) the Saar, (3) Danzig, (4) Memel, (5) Fiume. A number of these suggestions were made directly to Miller by Sir William Wiseman, the powerful figure behind the scenes in the British Foreign Office during the month preceding the formal opening of the Paris Conference, by Sir William Tyrell, earlier secretary to Sir Edward Grey, and by Sir Eustace Percy, to whom the British Government appears to have given over much of

tion cautiously undefined. No clearer understanding of the British view could be gained than that to be had by gleaning through the record of official and unofficial conversations contained in the monumental *Diary* of David Hunter Miller, Wilson's principal legal adviser on League matters. Here are the jottings of conversations with the leading lights of the British Empire Delegation at Paris: now a breakfast conference with Cecil, now a conversation with General Smuts, now a heart-to-heart talk with Sir Eustace Percy, and now the telltale marks of a duel of rapierlike minds as the gist of an afternoon's discourse with Sir Cecil Hurst, is put into record. All these are available to the public eye,—if you can get access to one of forty extant copies,—but there are more, many more, in the private files, that have never been printed. I believe I shall now be betraying no confidences if I say that this amazing record of colloid conversations from which Miller tried—not always successfully—to precipitate a substantial residuum, gives the clearest evidence of the alternate conception of an unwritten—or in large part unwritten—constitution for the whole field of international government.[3]

the exploratory work with respect to a League of Nations. The idea of not defining jurisdiction directly is clearly conveyed in one of Miller's earliest dispatches from London to Colonel House, dated December 3, 1918, recording Sir Eustace Percy's suggestion of putting the Straits under American mandate and his idea that "in this way, if similar agreements were generally reached, *the League of Nations would very largely have its functions determined without any attempt to formulate general principles.*" Miller frankly added: "I regard Percy's conversation as an effort *to convey to me without stating them as such,* some of the British ideas which have been formulated."—*My Diary at the Peace Conference of Paris,* I:27–28.

[3] Curiously, this conception was shared at the time by only one vocal American—David Jayne Hill, later one of President Wilson's most ardent oppo-

On the specific matter of territorial guarantees, the British likewise had an alternate conception—one of irreducible opposition. Their unfeigned reluctance to sponsor any such guarantees was entirely in character. The practice of absorbing various small states, both civilized and barbarous, by placing them, with or without an intervening war, "under the protection of Her [or His] Britannic Majesty," was an imperial habit much too deeply rooted to be lightly abandoned. It appears that the British were much more concerned with establishing the habit of resort to peaceful procedures than with any substantive guarantees to individual states. Without guarantees, but by firm insistence on pacific procedure, it was believed that peaceful change could be effected more reasonably all the way round. Hence the British preference for a perpetual flux, or colloid territorial status, than for the rigid territorial guarantees demanded by the French for historical and military reasons, and backed unflinchingly by Wilson,

---

nents, and in many ways one of the most reactionary, if also most realistic, students of international organization. Writing of the problem in 1917, he dismissed the pretension that a general international government was either possible or desirable, but believed possible a *compact* between a limited number of states acting as "a nucleus for the ultimate union of all responsible and socially inclined nations." "It would not necessarily be a federation, which would imply the creation of a new state, nor even an alliance. It might be in substance merely the formal recognition of the existence of a real, as distinguished from a purely fictitious, society of states based upon common intentions and a declaration of definite principles of right which the members were willing to accept, to observe and to defend." In order to keep this inchoate society from being "a mere fiction of the mind," Hill proposed vaguely to give it "some kind of legislative, judicial and executive powers," but he steadfastly denied that the establishment of new relations "was equivalent to the creation of a new entity": "There would be no new sovereignty developed, but merely the concurrent action of preexistent sovereignties."—*The Rebuilding of Europe* (1917), pp. 187–188.

even to the extent of a supplemental treaty of guarantee to France. What Wilson failed to read as a lesson out of our own national history was that the fixed guarantee of territory was reached by the United States constitutionally only at the federal, and not the confederal, stage,[4] and that if the territorial guarantees of the Constitution were to be carried over into the field of international government, the other indicia of federalism must likewise be present.

In the end, of course, Wilson was victorious; but not wholly so. In place of a League of amorphous structure and limited responsibilities but with well-nigh plenary powers, he got a written Covenant, with fixed territorial commitments, but a Covenant from which the British had astutely filtered out many distasteful jurisdictional encroachments once they saw it was predestined to be written.[5] It was left with the tragic combination of definite territorial guarantees and a vague and

---

[4] Actually, the Articles of Confederation merely provided a leaguing of the States "for their common defense, the security of their liberties and their mutual and general welfare"; they bound themselves to assist each other "against all force offered to, or attacks made upon them, or any of them, on account of religion, sovereignty, trade or any other pretence whatever" (Art. III). The idea of mutual support is clear, but, with doubtful boundaries so widely prevalent, no thought occurred of guaranteeing definite territory. Curiously the only guarantee was against loss of territory by a State to the United States! (Art. IX, par. 3).

[5] Miller records, apropos of the Hurst-Miller draft of the Covenant, his meeting with President Wilson and Colonel House on the night of February 2, 1919, to extenuate—apparently rather unconvincingly—the emasculated document: "I explained to the President what Mr. Hurst had said about Lloyd George's desire for brevity, and described generally how agreement on the paper had been reached. *The President said that he did not like the paper very much; that the British seemed to have taken a good many things out, some of which he thought were important*."—Diary, I:104–105. (Italics mine.— M. W. G.)

nebulous affirmative jurisdiction—"any matter concerning the peace of the world"—along with sharply defined negative jurisdiction, carefully excluding from discussion domestic questions, hedging about with well-nigh impossible restrictions all treaty-revision procedure, decentralizing the responsibility for territorial guarantees,[6] and leaving the whole structure at the mercy of individual or cumulative secession.

Meanwhile, much of the detailed, affirmative jurisdiction which the League might have claimed was in fact transferred to other independent bureaus, commissions, and tribunals, or vested in the International Labor Organization. The net result was a deconcentration of international authority, leaving the League to a large degree a political body rivaled in that field during immediate postwar days by the Supreme Council, and later by the Conference of Ambassadors,—a formal structure with impaired administrative jurisdiction, with no judiciary as yet an integral part of its mechanism, and with very many economic functions essential to international well-being relegated to another, and in a sense competitive, organism. Such was the skeletal structure of international organization at the hour of its birth.

Other losses than those produced by deconcentration of authority occurred in the process. Of these perhaps the most tragic came through the rejection of the Japanese amend-

---

[6] This was acknowledged by President Wilson when he told the Senate in a special message, July 29, 1919, that the territorial guarantees ordinarily became operative upon advice of the Council of the League—"advice given, it is to be presumed, only upon deliberation and acted upon by each of the Governments of the member states only if its own judgment justifies such action" (*Public Papers of Woodrow Wilson,* V:555). This is, of course, a completely confederal conception.

ment put forward in all sincerity by Baron Makino, an amendment which would have embodied racial equality as one of the cornerstones of the Covenant. Proposed as a rational counterpart to President Wilson's own project guaranteeing religious liberty and equality, it encountered strong resistance from Wilson and Cecil—paradoxically the vicarious representatives of militant Nordic Aryanism—and its rejection caused the equal refusal of religious guarantees. If in the postwar years there has been widespread *racial* intolerance, if in the present hour there is no less *religious* intolerance in large parts of the world, much responsibility therefor attaches to the refusal of an elemental right no less significant to the Hindu and Assyrian and the Finn than to the Turk or Japanese. The subsequent exaction of minority guarantees from new or enlarged states through treaties which operated unilaterally and did not establish a generally binding juridical régime, did not, to say the least, improve the situation. With so important a juridical pediment left out by the builders, the grand edifice of international government could not be expected to attain full symmetry.

It is, I feel sure, quite unnecessary for me to recall here the actual content of either the League Covenant or of those clauses of Part XIII of the Treaty of Versailles called at the time the "Labor Covenant." Suffice it to say that, like the later Statute of the Permanent Court of International Justice, both laid down—in virtue of their written character—specific and exact legal obligations expressly binding the signatory states. The product of meticulous drafting, they were carefully fashioned juridical instruments, as significant for the stipulations they laid down as for those which they omitted. I venture to state that at no time in human history has a political document been subjected to such severe scrutiny, such hard and close construction, as was the League Covenant. Precisely because it proclaimed itself to be a law of superior obligation, it was treated so rigorously, particularly by the small states which were anxious to avoid incurring extensive obligations, as in large measure to construe out of existence, or at least severely reduce the incidence of, the obligations assumed at the time of signature or accession. Herein has lain, and continues to lie, one of the gravest difficulties with, and deficiencies of, the existing scheme of world organization.

The evils of a decade of strict construction could not be overcome by the spirit of Locarno, and the right of nullification—i.e., of refusal by a state to carry out the agreed policy or course of action of the League—asserted with respect to sanctions in 1935 by Albania, Austria, Hungary, and Switzerland, merely went to prove that, if organized on a purely confederal basis, and precariously subject to the contrarient whims of an infinitesimal minority, the functioning of international political organization must be in permanent jeopardy. After the devitalizing right of secession was fully conceded at the outset by the Paris Peace Conference, the assumed right of nullification tacitly accepted at Geneva in 1935 was a staggering blow. To this has been added more recently the paralyzing effect of the rule of unanimity, which is proving as nefarious in effect in League annals as was the *liberum veto* in the days before the partitions of Poland; how definitely ruinous is amply illustrated by the effect of the adverse votes of Albania and Portugal on October 2, 1937, which blocked all League action in checking aggression in Spain.[7]

Clearly, international government and institutions are now at the crossroads, and, if only from strictly constitutional premises, it may reasonably be forecast that if the disintegrative processes now patent are not sharply arrested and the disruptive trend reversed, the dissolution of the political confederacy is all too likely. May I recur for confirmation to the analogy from our constitutional history and point out how highly critical our present epoch is in the development of institutions of world government.[8]

Perhaps it was inevitable that the institutions of international government must pass through the confederal stage. At the risk of being branded a Trotskist for borrowing from the deposed commissar the terminology of his "Law of Combined Development,"[9] may I suggest that it offers a clue to a historical possibility, that, if rightly manipulated at the outset,—by adopting, on English counsel, the essence of federalism without bothering to define jurisdictions,—international government might, from a juridical standpoint, have moved directly from chaos and anarchy toward viable federation. Realistically, we must concede that this was predestined not to be.

---

[7] *Records of the Eighteenth Assembly,* Plenary Sessions, October 2, 1937.

[8] To a lesser degree the foregoing is true of the Labor Covenant, although because of its narrower scope and more restricted authority as well as by reason of its more dynamic ideology, the damage inflicted has not been nearly so great: The Court Statute, having been framed to accept procedures of much longer standing, clearer context, and less contentious meaning, has suffered to only a slight degree from strict construction.

[9] Leon Trotsky, *History of the Russian Revolution,* I:6.

A deeper and more fundamental reason for the breakdown which we are now witnessing is to be found in the economic contexts of the international reorganization of 1919. Is it not somewhat ironic that, with Paris fairly shivering before the specter of Communism, which had raised red flags from Bokhara to Bavaria, the Covenant, and its cognate nexus of new legalities, were envisioned by Wilson and his Paris colleagues as almost wholly political, and virtually divorced from economic connotations? In the presence of manifest social and economic upheaval, the Right Wing of the international organizers proposed merely a return to the world of free trade and laissez faire, the economic ambient of 1914. In the League Covenant there was no stipulation to give adequate control over international commerce, equal access to raw materials, and so on. True to the confederal conception, the League abstained from impinging on the economic sovereignty of its constituent parts. Not that such suggestions were not known to the makers of the Covenant: from ultraconservative as well as from enemy,[10] labor, and radical circles,[11] the suggestions of control over commerce were proffered; but they were never accepted. Here once again is a stone which the builders rejected! In a word, the system of world political organization which the Founding Fathers sponsored at Paris in 1919 was

[10] Thus Chapter VI of the German official project for a League of Nations included a recognition that "an International Commercial Treaty" was to be the aim of the endeavors of the members of the League. Cf. D. H. Miller, *The Drafting of the Covenant*, II:745–761.

[11] Thus Morris Jastrow, the historian of the Bagdad railway, put first among the objectives of international organization the regulation of international commerce (*The War and the Coming Peace* [1918], p. 106). H. G. Wells (*In the Fourth Year: The League of Free Nations* [1918], p. 34) puts it second only to control over backward areas.

contingent upon a return to the *economic status quo ante bellum.*[12] It was based on a credo of economic liberalism which the postwar world, with its ardent and autarchic nationalism, has steadfastly rejected; we can now see in retrospect that the postwar world has in reality been attempting to reconcile two incompatibles. Small wonder, then, that we today can grasp, in the limited historical perspective of less than two decades, the inherent contradiction which has existed throughout the period between the postulates of the economic policy of the constituent states and the principles implicit in the political organization established. In pointing out this contradiction I am, confessedly, breaking no new ground. Unlike the idealists, however, I feel that a sense of realities should make us aware of the fact that this unrepentant world has refused to be cast back into its 1914 economic mold. More, perhaps, than any other single thing, this endeavor to bend the world to an economic pattern from which it has palpably departed has been responsible for the hiatus between the beautiful blueprint of the structure of international government and the

---

[12] Indeed, there is evidence in the unpublicized minutes of the Baltic Commission of the Paris Peace Conference that, after negotiating with Kolchak, Wilson and his colleagues were, for a historical moment, disposed to use the League as an instrument to ratify and sanctify the Russian counterrevolution, i.e., to return politically, in that quarter of the globe, to the *status quo ante* (*Conférence des Préliminaires de Paix, Commission des Affaires Baltiques, Procès-Verbal No. 12*, July 2, 1919, pp. 16–17). That the effort did not succeed ought not to be attributed either to the timidity of Allied statesmanship or the weakness of the White armies. In the words of John A. Hobson, "The notion of the League turning into a new Holy Alliance of the Capitalist bureaucracy within each state for the concerted repression of all democratic movements can hardly be a serious apprehension in face of the divergencies of interest between the ruling groups within the several states."—*Democracy after the War* (1919), p. 209.

sordid economic hovels in which, for better or for worse, the world continues to live.

Of planned economy, of the rationalization of international economic life, the organism set up by the League Covenant had scarcely a touch. Its charter was filled with humanitarian concern over the maltreatment of backward peoples, and had, along with moral encomiums, excellent suggestions for their better governance and the retention of their primitive economy; but, in essence, all the Covenant did was to repeat the shibboleths of the Anti-Slavery and Aborigines Protection Societies of the 1840's. Its was the liberalism of anarchy, not of order in economic life.

On the other hand, the Left Wing of the international organizers, led by such "radicals" as the late Samuel Gompers and my distinguished fellow citizen, Mr. Henry M. Robinson, elaborated the Labor Covenant in terms of a dynamic and expanding industrialized society with the recurring necessity of fundamental adjustments consensually arrived at between capital and labor. That is why the International Labor Organization, which got under way much sooner and has at all times grappled much more thoroughly with the realities of the economic situation, made so much more progress and developed such palpable momentum. If it has at times exhibited too obvious an acquaintance with the tears and sweat of an industrial society, it has at all events never been redolent, as has now and then been true of the *Palais des Nations,* of the fragrance of lavender and old lace.

Without wishing to exaggerate the differences between the two bodies, I do wish to lay emphasis upon the realism of the International Labor Organization—a Hamiltonian body which has linked both the vested interests of entrepreneurs and the passionate beliefs of a large part of the Western proletariat to the successful working of its peaceful machinery of continuous economic accommodation, as contrasted with the studied Jeffersonianism of the League, and the view that the least international action is best. To the International Labor Organization belongs the credit of having sensed in advance the value of social planning, of extracting from the contemporary wave of guild socialism the principle of employer-and-employee representation, of building up a disciplined personnel and a technique for noncontentious handling of complex, crucially difficult, economic questions. It is no small satisfaction to see the Government of the United States associated in this promotion of the general welfare on a world-wide scale which, in the language of our Chief Executive, is at the same time a principal insurance of our common domestic tranquillity.

But today in this world no nation can be tranquil. It has not been enough to develop through the Covenant, the Permanent Court of International Justice, and hundreds of arbitration and conciliation treaties practical procedures for pacific settlement, and rational arguments for their voluntary adoption. We are faced with the problem of the states which are not bound by the pledges of the Genevan society, and which own no obligation to enter the Peace Palace at The Hague. They are at large in the world and acknowledge no limitations on their sovereignty, either of the hoary consuetudinal variety or of the contract concluded in political fair weather.

These not only put to the test the institutions and procedures of the League, but also strain the ancillary structures of international law and society. Yet, paradoxically enough, they are strengthened, in their defiance of the societal law, by their formal departure from the Confederacy of the Covenant after an interval of respite in which the preëxisting law was allowed to go into desuetude. For, with the expectations of prompt attainment of universality which accompanied the birth of an assumedly new world order, the older practices were regarded as obsolete, as outmoded, even as contemnable. Hence the defiant state today finds itself freed from old and customary trammels, particularly of the laws of war when there is no declared war, while because of the ease of exodus from the confederation it has hitherto been unlikely to undergo constraint.

That the absolutist state was the principal barrier on the road to international organization was fully foreseen by writers in the pre-Covenant period. Thus David Jayne Hill, perhaps as well versed as any American in the diplomacy of absolutism, wrote: "It is evident that autocratic powers, basing their authority upon the postulates of absolutism, will not and logically cannot accept this view of essentially limited state authority and the consequent existence of inherent and binding international obligations, for the reason that these limitations and obligations are, from their point of view, encroachments upon the unlimited will of the sovereign. . . . If, as the absolutist theory of the state contends, the sovereignty of the state is unlimited, such a state is bound only by its will, which is casual and changeable. Its will to reject an obligation is as absolute as its will to accept it." Then, in order to draw attention to the need of concerted action, he pointed out why such absolutist conceptions must necessarily set at naught the will of the remaining members of the international community: "No treaty can bind them for they always reserve the right to break it whenever they consider it in their interest to do so. No international law can control them for they will not admit that it is a law.... No congress or conference can overrule them, for these, in their view, possess no authority. All contractual relations entered into with powers which hold themselves not subject to moral [shall we say the societal?] law are therefore written in running water." In essence, the claim to "liberty of national development"—a phrase much in vogue in the Wilhelmstrasse at the time when Hill wrote— meant nothing "if not freedom to do what a particular nation desires to do *without the restraint of the collective interests of other powers and the limitations imposed by fixed principles of law*."[18] The challenge of which Hill wrote was that of the Hohenzollerns, but it has no less meaning today when applied to the three authoritarian empires that tug at the leashes of international legality.

What is the likelihood of restraint by the "collective interests of other Powers?" For answer we are once again driven to conclude that a stone which the builders rejected in 1919 must sooner or later be retrieved at great cost from the quarry of oblivion—this time the ideological concept of an international police force, military, naval, and aerial, to stand as the safeguard of the societal life against the irresponsible or absolutist state. I, for one, do not wish to underestimate the dif-

---

[18] *The Rebuilding of Europe*, pp. 180–183. (Italics mine.—M. W. G.)

ficulties of restraint and coercion of a state or states palpably
bent on breaking the common peace; I merely wish to point
out that the events of the last three years have given a grim-
mer aspect of realism and foresight to the French proposals
for a general staff to place effective sanctions immediately
at the service of the international community—proposals dismissed in the hour of victory, when the relations of power
seemed favorably fixed, as "chimerical," "fantastic," or "pre-
posterous," and because they tended to be antidemocratic! On
this issue the protagonists of the new international order
divided sharply in 1919; to this day there is a great gulf fixed
between them.

But what then gave great cogency to the Anglo-American
view against sanctions and an international force was the expectation that the interval of peace which Allied victory had
vouchsafed could be more effectively utilized in building up
the procedures of peace and loyalties to its institutions than
in devising means of collective coercion and constraint. Today that historical interval lies behind us, and not ahead, and
we are face to face with the reality that the procedures of
peace are violated, and that nascent loyalties to the world
community have been offset by the pressure in more than one
quarter of dynamic yet contrarient political dogmas. Strange
paradox that the feared alignment of the new order, in 1919,
against the forces of the Left, is taking place, with far greater
fervor, against the forces of the Right which have reverted to
the bluffing and saber-rattling traditionally associated with
power politics, now militantly organized in the service of
an anti-international and antidemocratic ideology! And yet

the process is not an irrational one: it rests upon a vast, amorphous, and pervasive desire in human relations for the vindication of justice and an equal urge to anticipatory self-preservation. Speaking twenty-one years ago on this very problem, seen in its contemporary contexts, Benjamin Ide Wheeler declared: "Advance [after strife and war] comes only by the intrusion of time and wider consideration in the place of impulse and inconsiderate violence. Then the reasonableness begotten of time may strike the balance we call justice. For the recognition of justice we must have the check of time, and for time we must have, so far as we know the mood of human affairs, the check of power. What we need to find is some form of expressible innate power in human society which will induce the recognition of justice."[14] I cannot find anywhere in the vast literature on our subject a more cogent, classic statement of the problem. Today we are not vouchsafed, as was an isolationist generation nearly two decades ago, the check of time. Both for the institutions of international government and for us as a people, it is the inexorable choice of finding the check of power.

Significantly, an approach is only now being made, under the pressure of crisis, on the naval side. At long last, after nearly twenty years of evasion, the issue of the rôle to be played by sea power in the framework of international government has come to the forefront of international politics. The issue has received little clarification, mainly because of the inflexible decision of the British and French foreign offices

[14] "Enforced Peace," *Proceedings of the First Annual National Assemblage of the League to Enforce Peace,* Washington, May 26–27, 1916, p. 81.

in the closing days of the World War not to allow the problem to be raised at all. Thus the ticklish Second Point in the Wilsonian catalogue, dealing alike with freedom and closure of the seas,[15] was conveniently dropped by the Allies before even armistice was discussed in 1918, and with it all thought of linking sea power to the service of international organization. That is why sea power was eventually discussed and prorated at Washington and London, but never by the League. The merest intimation that the British fleet might have to be employed to uphold the principles of the Geneva Protocol was one of the causes that unleashed the political avalanche in Great Britain in the fall of 1924, buried Macdonald and Henderson beneath it for half a decade, and led to a number of ill-starred, backstairs proposals like the Anglo-French conversations of 1927–1928. Not even the crisis in the Orient in 1931–1932 was allowed to involve sea power, however remotely, nor was Great Britain willing to discuss it in connection with sanctions in 1935.

Only as the immediate risks of the Mediterranean have arisen during the Spanish civil war has the linking of sea power to international organization been more closely envisaged. It is not wholly without irony that the question, in the postwar period, was posed first at Washington, then at London, then at Montreux, and now, most recently, at Nyon— almost at a stone's throw from the League's portals. In the bridging of the psychological distances, progress has also been

---

[15] "II. Absolute freedom of navigation upon the seas, outside territorial waters, alike in peace and in war, except as the seas may be closed in whole or in part by international action for the enforcement of international covenants."— *The Public Papers of Woodrow Wilson*, V:159.

made. Although it would be premature to say that an organic liaison has been effected between naval power and international organization, certainly the way toward it is now open and the Anglo-French antipiracy fleets in the Mediterranean are in fact exercising a naval mandate on behalf of much more than the immediate riverain states. I think we may safely say that as a result of very bitter experience, and the realization that naval power cannot be allowed to be antisocially exercised, the stone which the builders of 1919 rejected *a priori* in 1918 is in a fair way to become a cornerstone of any set of viable institutions of international government.

A second approach to the check of power has been made on the economic side. After theoretical discussion, in 1920–1921, of the potential uses of "the economic weapon," no actual occasion for its implementation arose for a decade—not until the Manchurian crisis. Then hesitatingly discussed, the project of employing it was abandoned until the Ethiopian war again brought home the necessity of preventing an irresponsible state from continuing in a predatory, antisocial way. It is significant that the imposition of sanctions in 1935 constituted the first effort in history to organize in the interests of the international community the cumulative economic power of some fifty states. That effort, though marred by imperfect enforcement and local nullification, was successful as pressure, but not swift enough as deterrent, and was abandoned, more, I venture to say, on political grounds than from intrinsic shortcomings. Today, in the presence of several simultaneous crises, renewed efforts are being made to put into effect the coercive machinery that is at hand. The immediate present has witnessed a marked taking of courage, a new impetus to the utilization of the economic weapon. An offending party has been designated and, on League initiative, the problem has been turned over to the nine Powers having a regional understanding for the maintenance of peace in the Pacific, with the Grotian admonition to all not to do anything which may hurt the injured party nor to aid, in any way, the aggressor. While still decentralized, as is the coercive power of any confederacy, the course now being charted for the new endeavor has vast potentialities as a check to irresponsible power. What the actual outcome will be, is veiled by the future. Perhaps by the conjoint use of economic pressure and a partial closure—at comfortably long range—of the seas, there may be opportunity to discover what even a crippled confederacy can do in an hour of critical emergency.

Twenty years are but a short span in the history of institutions, yet those of world organization, for all their obvious imperfection, have made progress. There have been definite drawbacks: the failure to form a union sufficiently strong to withstand disintegrative pressures; marked weakness in the scope and methodology of safeguarding what we may call the International Bill of Rights; breakdown, at times, of measures for the common defense against aggression. Opposite these must be registered indisputable gains in the widespread establishment of means to advance the general welfare, and much zealous work to enhance the internal tranquillity of our several societies. We have witnessed the creation of flexible instrumentalities for the prompt attainment of justice between socially minded States, and the inception, if only the merest beginnings, of the socially imperative check to arbitrary power. Decidedly, we have not moved in the single leap which the immediate postwar world envisioned from the European and World Anarchy of 1914 to the Parliament of Man and the Federation of the World. The present period is indeed critical, but, if the crisis is surmounted, the turn will not be back to anarchy but on toward a more perfect union. At the moment we can only say that we have all been witnesses or participants in the starting of the institutions, and are now experiencing the implementing of the processes, in which are bound up the hope and the very life of the Great Society.

IS WORLD PEACE
AN ATTAINABLE IDEAL?

———

GEORGE M. STRATTON

PROFESSOR OF PSYCHOLOGY, EMERITUS
IN THE UNIVERSITY OF CALIFORNIA

Lecture delivered October 27, 1937

IS WORLD PEACE
AN ATTAINABLE IDEAL?

I

NONE OF US wishes to be quixotic in his international aims. There is so much of sane work waiting in our troubled world, so much that is important and within our powers, that we should gladly keep our hands at these, and turn away from what is at once alluring and impossible.

So we will examine the proposal to have world peace, and attempt to judge whether this lies at the rainbow's end. Or does it, rather, belong with human flying, or speech across oceans,—things long unrealized, declared to be impossible to realize, and then made real. If there are solid reasons for holding that a warless world is incredible, let us know them and turn—sadder and perhaps wiser—to other things. Is, then, world peace, as the older Moltke believed, a mere dream?

Our decision may depend largely on the form we give to this ideal. For it takes different shapes in the mind.

World peace means for some a world in which there can be no war. The ideal, for such persons, is of a mankind that has reached a quality of life not only far beyond what has yet been attained in the society of nations as a whole, but far beyond what has yet been attained by any member nation in that society. In the United States, for example, there is and always has been lawless violence by individuals, and we have had states in rebellion against the federal government, which the government labored years to suppress. Much as we pray that no revolt in our country will ever occur again, it is not impossible. Likewise, in the British Commonwealth of Nations there is crime, and rebellion has not been unknown; and against our strongest hope, it may occur again. The Commonwealth and the Union have great power to control their citizens, their member peoples, and yet even here the peace is not an inviolable peace.

Or again, the ideal may be not only of a degree of peace beyond what is found in any large community, but of peace to be kept without those means which all our actual large communities have always felt compelled to use. The world of nations, in this ideal, is to be without visible government, without court of law, or police. The community world-wide would be of nations living in an unviolent orderly anarchy.

Only the family or the small chosen fellowship has ever attained this kind of peace. Good-will and self-control, indispensable in all orderly companies great or small, have never been enough even in our nation, which has sought to hold compulsion down to its lowest terms and raise liberty to its highest. Our polity would fail, we believe, without a government prepared to define our several rights and obligations, to adjudge and redress violations, to defend both the weak and the strong against the reckless and the malevolent.

Now a world order with both or either of these two characters seems to me hardly worth long attention. I do not look to see such an order come. Even Milton, political thinker as well as Puritan and poet, did not conceive God's kingdom to be incapable of rebellion. Even less did he conceive it to be unorganized, ungoverned. And so for myself the way leads whither, I believe, it must have led in Milton's thinking about this world,—leads not to a noble anarchy nor to a society in which there can be no revolt, no breaking of law. Such an ideal, in my judgment, needs no more of our time; there is so slight a probability that it will ever be attained.

A different ideal is already suggested,—of a world at peace because it has become a greater community not essentially unlike one of the great political communities we know,— Sweden, Switzerland, Great Britain, France, Canada, or the United States,—with government perhaps of some new form, as the United States government was a new form, and as the British Commonwealth under the Statute of Westminster is a new form today. The ideal which I would ask to be allowed to examine with you will by no means turn its back on all that is better than the nations have yet created, but it would be born in imperfection and with the way open for advance. Peace as I conceive it will not come entire or not at all. There can be less of it, or more. Our country has peace within its borders, but has little beyond the rudiments of peace. Denmark and England and Switzerland have more.

The knotty problem for us, then, is this: Is it possible to have nations, in their conduct toward one another, dominated by a common will for order under law, and not by private violence, a communal order at first no nearer its goal than what is now in the better actual political communities? Can the nations as a whole come to an organized readiness to work together for the common welfare, somewhat as do the Swiss cantons, or the member nations of the British Commonwealth, or the States of our own Union? The League of Nations as conceived by Smuts, Cecil, and Wilson, would also illustrate the object of our inquiry. We shall not feel tempted, I am sure, to confuse this ideal of a world in the beginnings of political order with a world perfect in all respects—perfect in its economics, medicine, law, education, fine arts, manners and morals, and religion. This, again, is in no country of our world, not even the best. A world which kept the peace through law and through good-will in nine of every ten nations, would not have these, but would have the way open for a more determined advance toward them than is possible where war must be in the center of each nation's mind.

An ideal like this will to some seem no ideal at all, but only the maundering of crass realism. Yet even this moderate ideal—for it is an ideal, I must think—will seem to many an unattainable ideal. The obstacles in its way, they believe, are insuperable. We now come to our task.

Is this defeatist judgment right or wrong? There cannot at once be a plain Yes or No. We shall have to fetch a wide compass, with soundings and a sharp lookout; we must explore the many obstacles, appraise their height, see also what powers we have to surmount them and what motives there are for setting ourselves resolutely to the work.

II

What are the most important of the obstacles? We shall find a formidable array of them. And first let us have before us the obstacles that seem fixed, like mountain ranges, in the very nature of things. These and the obstacles that are man-made will not be appraised until after they have passed in rapid review.

At the head of the array comes what belongs, not to psychology alone, but to all biology, the struggle for existence. This, by writers who out-Darwin Darwin, is seen as the central principle of international life, and warfare as the form this struggle takes among nations. Warfare is thus regarded as the greatest if not the sole means by which the better nations are chosen and the worse are left, an inescapable force for the world's good.

Next come certain inborn traits in mankind and in many of the animals below man,—a native readiness to feel aversion, to be angry, to fight. War, it is held, is this reaction become a reaction of men in the mass,—in the clan, the tribe, or the nation. Racial prejudice is named among these native reactions of men, an antipathy toward those who are not of our stock, which leads to war and helps to make war ineradicable in the intercourse between race and race. The feeling between Occident and Orient, between Italian and Abyssinian, is thus seen as the outburst of deep forces, the hot volcanic forces in our nature.

Often these particular inborn forms of reaction—instinctive racial prejudice, instinctive anger, instinctive pugnacity—are summed up in the term 'human nature.' Human nature, it is felt, will forever defeat all attempts to have men live at peace with one another; human nature has always defeated it, and human nature never changes. A similar thought is expressed in other words. In a book on *The Psychology of War,* written by an officer of the United States army, General Eltinge, and published by our Government for the instruction of its soldiers, we find: "Civilization is but skin-deep," and "Scratch a civilized man and find a savage." The real man, in this view, is affected only on the surface by the effort of the family, school, religion, and state, to make him humane. The real man is inalterably a savage and a killer.

But no catalogue of the barriers against orderly life among nations is complete that includes only those that come from nature. There are others quite as real, perhaps as difficult to move. They are made by man. He himself builds walls which prevent him from seeing squarely some of his fellows, from feeling with them, and working with them. These, too, are barriers to peace, because they make more difficult if not impossible the coming of that sense of common interests, of common resources, outer and inner, which are indispensable for the joint effort by which the desired world order can become real.

The name of these man-made creatures is legion. My selection from among them all can be but a sample.

A name perhaps as good as any for them all might be 'national prejudice,' the counterpart of racial prejudice. It is the antipathy so often evident between certain nations,—between France and Germany, between Germany and Russia, between Russia and Japan, between Japan and China. It has its degrees; and in some low degree at least, and in some particular direction, it is nearly universal. We ourselves are not wholly without national prejudice.

In nations it is like electricity, having two poles. I have just illustrated only its negative pole, its repulsion, its passionate opposition to a people under another government than our own, a prejudice *against*. At its positive pole is also a prejudice, but now a prejudice *for*, for ourselves. This is the national self-esteem which is a part of health in national life. No nation can live without valuing itself in some degree. This is needed to give the nation solidarity, organized strength. It does not come naturally, it comes by art; it must be stimulated. And to make sure that the nation has enough, it is over-stimulated, and what is needed psychologically to balance it is neglected or is drugged into sleep, until we have in the end the monstrous self-love which makes many a nation fairly impossible to work with, and indeed dangerous to be at large. The nation's self-valuing completely blinds it to the value of its neighbor nations; its own interests alone have a call upon its powers. If these interests can be furthered by deceit, seizure of another's land, the bombing of cities with their civilian men, women, and children, such action seems justified. Even in its milder degrees, which no nation can forego, this self-esteem disturbs the judgment, so that the nation fondly sees itself as peace-loving beyond all other nations, as waging only righteous wars, as higher-minded and, if not exactly the chosen people, at least the choicest of all peoples in the world.

Let us look more intently at this national prejudice with its two poles, of prejudice for ourselves and of prejudice against others. We shall notice aspects of it that deserve to be named separately. They overlap. We have no need here of nice distinction.

There is *patriotism*, which is psychologically of one blood with *nationalism*,—patriotism having its wide range of temperature from tepid to boiling and then on to degrees which could be gauged only by a pyrometer. Patriotism has also various breadths and sincerities, ranging from what we find in Lincoln down to what was in the eye of Samuel Johnson when he declared patriotism to be the last refuge of a scoundrel. A certain quality in those who are aptly called 'patriots for profit' should not be overlooked. In some degree and in its best quality no nation can do without patriotism; while in some other degree and quality it is very pest in international life. 'Nationalism' is the word for the high temperatures, the divisive features of patriotism.

Another obstacle is *sovereignty,* which is the cold fact that nations are politically independent, each politically supreme like a sovereign. They know no government over them, they live in a virtual anarchy around them.

While sovereignty is a cold fact, it must be named among the warm things in national self-esteem. Thus it comes into the field of psychology. For the fact does not remain an external fact; it is recognized, treasured, acclaimed. The independence marked by the brave term 'sovereignty' becomes a vested national interest, emotionally guarded, its slightest diminution resisted as though it meant the break-up of the whole national structure. Sovereignty, thus converted into a national treasure, almost into a national idol, resists the changes, the approach toward organization, essential to peace.

Autarchy also is among these obstacles. It is not a fact, like sovereignty, but is what some would make a fact. There is already, indeed, a good measure of separation of nations—in their production, commerce, and finance. The autarchists would take this and make it greater, to the last possible pitch. To whatever degree they succeed, by so much is the chasm between nations widened, and the task is made harder of bringing them a little closer together, to set their hands at the common work.

Finally, as a part or as a display of national prejudice, comes the *double standard of conduct.* For the behavior of individuals toward individuals is almost universally judged by a different standard from that used for the behavior of nations toward nations. In our personal relations, there is approval of truth-telling, of respect for others' possessions and for others' lives. The opposites of these are disapproved,—lying, stealing, homicide. And with the disapproval goes disgrace. But when men's minds move out into the region of national conduct, then suddenly from some cupboard of the mind comes an entirely different standard, and a man is praised and rewarded for deeds that between individuals would blacken his name. Men are decked out in most honored vestments and are given high titles, to go forth and deliberately seize others' land, burn their dwellings, and slaughter them and their families.

Now this low level of international conduct, fostered by this perverse standard of judging it, is not merely a matter of moral regret, it blocks the way to peace. For peace can be reached only by constructive collaboration. And collaborators must believe one another and be without fear that one's fellow worker will stab one to the heart. International coöperation, so difficult even at the easiest, becomes tenfold more difficult because some nations' solemn pledge is worthless; after fair words, they rain bombs on a fellow nation's capital; they do their best to destroy its government and the nation itself. This is done by the proudest of ill-behaved nations. But even in the best-behaved, the sense of honor and obligation is far below that of their own individuals. A common belief is that a nation is above the moral law. Peace has this among so many other powerful currents against it. Its course is upstream.

III

Some of the forces opposed to peace have been named. They are many and formidable. Are they forbidding? Do they effectually, now and always, veto our enterprises? We must estimate their strength to resist.

Some of the obstacles which, it is thought, are created by nature, are not precisely what they are described to be. Or men have reasoned loosely from what these are.

What Darwin meant by "the struggle for existence" (to consider this for a moment) is true enough. But the reasoning from this truth to unending international war is unrigorous. Darwin's phrase, in the hands of those who support this war-idea, is given a special meaning which neither Darwin nor the facts of nature would approve. The struggle is taken to mean literally fighting, and only fighting. Now plants and animals are not always fighting, and their struggle for life is not usually a combat literally. Certain insects win in the struggle, not because they are good fighters but because they taste bad, or can hide, or can procreate more than enough to make good their losses. Our quail, our hummingbirds do not survive by outfighting eagles. The monkeys owe their continued existence not to defeating lions in open combat, but largely by their intelligence and dexterity used to avoid such combats. The apes do not ape the tigers. Nations too proud to use their brains for peace need not blame nature. Nature compels them neither to go to war nor to keep the peace. They may choose. The problem is one of intelligence, of political engineering.

Race prejudice as an obstacle is real but ill-described. It is not what it is said to be. Race prejudice, by the best evidence we have, is not nature-made but man-made. It is not an instinct, but a habit.

Nature's part in the matter is this: various stocks of men have been given various builds of body and a varying look of eye, hair, and skin, and probably some differences in their nervous and mental powers; and men have also been given the power to dislike. Now man himself, not nature, has taken the dislike and has attached it to the men of a stock differing from his own; and quite reasonably, because he or his ancestors have usually had unpleasant experience with them. If they do not fight him, they are found to be uncomfortable to have around; their manners, morals, loyalties are not agreeable. Race prejudice is not found in little children; they acquire it today from moving pictures, playmates, books, and parents. It is an obstacle, for all that, to international understanding; but nature has no sole hand in making it. It is man-made and can be unmade by man.

Nor is race prejudice as strong for war today as some think. Wars today are waged regardless even of the greatest differences of stock. White Italians, it is true, fight black Abyssinians, and yellow Japanese fight White Russians or Red Russians. But yellow Japanese are as ready to fight with yellow

Chinese; indeed they are now at their third war with them in fifty years. Our own six wars, in a little more than a century and a half, were all with men of our own Caucasian race. Germans and French are Caucasians. The World War, in the main, was within a single great stock. War does not stand or fall with race prejudice.

The opinion that war must always be, because we have in us instinctive pugnacity, is as ill-based on facts and as illogical as the opinion about racial prejudice. Anger, it is true, is natural to us, as are also our movements of struggle to overcome bodily restraint. But like racial prejudice, war is man-made, not nature-made. It is acquired. It rests on what is natural; but so does every habit, every reaction we acquire. Tobacco smoking is based on the native impulse or instinct to breathe and to suck; yet it is a habit, it is acquired. The use of the English language is based on the native power in the infant to make vocal sounds; yet the language has to be learned. We learn to smoke, speak English, and go to war;— learn to direct our natural powers into novel forms.

Indeed, the soldier's behavior is the very opposite of behavior by instinct. In it he takes his natural impulses and beats them into submission. He holds by the throat his natural fear of death, his natural impulse to rest when fatigued, his natural repugnance toward heat, cold, stench, and terrific noise. And this he can do only because he has learned to obey and to be loyal. War, in a strict psychological sense, is a habit. This kind of action is not to be ended by renaming it. The habit still holds as an obstacle to peace. But habits have been broken, and our problem has assumed a hopeful form.

The obstacle in unchanging human nature is the most widely regarded of the natural occasions for despair of peace.

Now it seems to be probable that human nature, as psychologists define it, has not changed importantly in the many thousand years from Cro-Magnon man to the man of the present day. Human culture has changed almost beyond our imagining; the use and fruits of man's native powers have changed; but the native powers themselves are probably what they were, thousands of years ago.

So this must never be out of mind, that even though our nature, in the psychologist's sense, may not change, this does not prevent profound changes in human thinking, human conduct, human institutions. Institutions which had their roots deep in our original constitution, to which men once clung as passionately as to life itself,—the feud with its blood-vengeance, human sacrifice in religion, human slavery,—these and more have been uprooted from the civilized world. It was not necessary to change human nature to uproot these poisonous things. Nor, probably, shall we need to change human nature to be rid of war. The problem of riddance, it is true, has not thereby been solved. But the problem has changed its face. It no longer requires us to do what demonstrably cannot be done.

The way is open. And what is even more encouraging, the way has already been followed far toward its end. To see the length of this journey, to see the solid successes attained, is better than a thousand abstractions. Most of us do not recognize what we have already won in our work for world peace.

The world has gone far in the control of fighting among

individuals. The boy in any civilized community gradually brings under control his fighting impulse, induced to do this by his playmates, his family, his entire community. His untamed physical efforts to repel and injure his opponent become obedient to a code among boys—in our English-speaking lands, not to bite, kick, or scratch, not to hit below the belt, not to strike a fellow when he's down, not to take a fellow of less than one's own size, not to fight with a cripple, not to attack a girl. It is a marvelous code, and, more, it is respected.

And then as the lad comes of age, the lusty fighter, without knowing it, turns pacifist. In all the area of his individual affairs, he has fought his last fight. Not that his passions have subsided. He still may scowl, turn pale, clench his fists, and in his rage say the unsayable. But he does not strike.

The change in girls, when we understand it, is even more remarkable. For it is against greater odds. Girls, our evidence indicates, in spite of their calmer mien, are intenser in their anger than are boys. But at an earlier age the girl stops her physical combats. She never again is free to scratch, slap, and kick; in a practical sense, she is pacified. She may be hotly angry, but her anger, her scorn, takes other forms of expression. "'Avin' no wish to quarrel, Mrs. R.," says the large woman to her neighbor, in *Punch,* "I'll say no more abaht yer, but you're welcome to read me thoughts." This is hardly in the spirit of the angels, but it is not physical violence; it is well along the way to be civilized.

Most citizens, even where crime runs high, have learned, if not to love their enemies, yet to hate them with respect. In

Chicago, for example, where passion often goes into killing, the men who do not kill, who control their impulses, are as thousands to one of those who lack this control. These thousands, in all affairs between themselves and other individuals, are practicing pacifists.

Nor is this pacification confined to the behavior of men singly. Great progress has been made in the behavior of group toward group. The family feud, which once flourished in our Southern mountains as in other backwaters of the world, is now rare with us. And where once there was warfare between city and city,—in Greece, Italy, Germany, and elsewhere,— cities now live at peace with neighbor cities.

And larger bodies of men, long at war with one another, have come to live at peace. France during her long history has seen the armies of her nobles arrayed in battle against one another. What is now England was for long the scene of warring kingdoms of the English themselves; and the Welsh and English fought each other; and the Scots had their warfare of clan with clan, and of highland with lowland Scots, and together they fought the English. But at length the area within which war was effectually prohibited was enlarged, until wars virtually ended in all Great Britain. And a like enlargement of the pacified area created Italy, Germany, and Japan. The old behavior of organized warfare was, in all these and many other lands, pushed out and out,—out of the city, out of the clan and the many neighboring clans, out beyond the duchy, beyond the principality, the petty kingdom, out over the border of the nation, of the confederation, or of the empire. The human effort for peace did not begin in the nineteenth century,—fostered by peace societies. It runs through history, with immense accomplishment now before our eyes. Its great results may give us heart. World peace is but a late stage of a long historic journey. The obstacles thought to be embedded in all living nature, and particularly in mankind, have thus far not blocked the way,—at least, not for any great length of time, nor completely.

IV

The degree of success just described says more than this. It speaks also of obstacles already named,—unbalanced national self-esteem, with its patriotism, nationalism, the cherishing of independence or sovereignty, its double standard and the accompanying low level of international morality. These were named, but not appraised in their final power of resistance. All these, or their psychological equivalents, have hotly opposed the enlargement of the warless areas, but have had to give way. They have been dislodged and required to move outward by a steady pressure of events, including a pressure of will.

We shall not be confused by mere names. In the Scottish clans, loyalty to clan and chieftain burned as hot against other clans and other chieftains as does the loyalty which today we know as patriotism in France, Denmark, or Japan. The object of the sentiment was different, but the sentiment itself had all its present fire. The same pride of independence that now is in Great Britain was once in separate Wales, separate Scotland, and separate England. The old prerogatives of sovereignty were then jealously guarded, as now. Autarchy in fact, though not in name, was sought in the German cities that once had their own armies, their water supply within the walls, their granaries filled against siege. In Peiping there is an eminence within the walled region known as the Tartar City, an eminence called Coal Hill, made, it is said, by a ruler who would have fuel when his city should be invested by the enemy. Words come and go, but the mind is less mobile. Yet these old aims and sentiments have not prevented the enlargement of the community.

And so it has been with nationalism. Some historians have liked to tell us that it is recent, as they measure time and as they define the word. But its psychological equivalent is old, and has had to yield. Men were zealots for their own political body long ago,—in Sweden, Denmark, Scotland; in Athens, Sparta, and Judea. The political zeal for the one people against all others flared up, scorched neighbors, was fought down and carried to new frontiers. Nor is the double standard and the present degraded level of international morals a new thing. The double standard has always been, and international morals have, time and again, been at low-water low. The obstacle these have been to the advance have slowed it but have not been able to stop it.

Indeed none of the obstacles which have been in review— neither obstacles clearly man-made nor obstacles in nature— have had strength to prevent the degree now attained of taming men as individuals, and of taming them in large bodies. There seems no insuperable obstacle to the advance still to be made before the world is under some larger measure of law and justice and good-will.

v

But all this is largely negative. No great social structure, such as world peace, will arise merely because there are no insuperable obstacles to erecting it. It cannot become a reality unless there are foundations for it in human nature at least as solid as those which have supported through all these thousands of years the institution of war.

It is time that we meant something fairly definite by 'human nature.' And let us mean by it the whole bundle of powers which come to us by biological inheritance, our various inborn powers to eat, sleep, see, think, to be stirred emotionally, to desire, and to act by the conscious guidance we call purpose or will,—all these apart from the various effects upon them, during a lifetime, from without and from within. Now among these are the powers which give whatever of natural basis there is for the activities we are not proud of in our fellow men—robbery, lying, bribery, murder, and war. But there are also powers which give what natural basis there is for acceptable activities, even admirable activities, such as agriculture, the exchange of goods, and the care of children; along with the art of healing, of judgment by law, of worship, of deliberating in assembly, and of keeping the peace. These acceptable things could not be, if men were not by nature given the power to like men as well as to dislike them, to mate and to associate amicably with others, as well as to hate and quarrel with them, to build as well as to destroy, to work with others in hunting, tilling, and navigation, and not only in war.

Indeed war itself would be impossible if men were not naturally sociable, given to the life of the family, the village, and the tribe, from which come city and state. An army, even an army of savages, is a body of coöperators, and has as its foundation the natural readiness to associate with others and to share in their interests. Peace must exist within the army, in order to create the army and to give it morale, even as peace today must exist behind the army to support it. For we here mean by peace, not mere idleness, not the mere absence of physical violence, but the fundamental ordering of a society by which there is opportunity to be busied, alone or with others, in food getting, food making, the building of house and home, in the training of young, and in a hundred other activities that bring reward. Peace, in fact, makes war possible, and has broader natural foundations than war. It calls more of man's native powers into action, and gives them freer play. Our enlarged structure of peace thus has bedrock on which to stand.

It is by a strange perversity that we so often see only deceit, lust, and cruelty at the core of man's being, calling these the real man, and calling ourselves, when we see them, realists. This is a form of negative hallucination, well known in hypnotism, in which the patient cannot mentally see what is plain before his eyes. The hospital, the university, and the cathedral are not creatures in the clouds, without basis in natural man. They, too, are products of our native powers, by training come into their own. Realism become scientific sees that these splendid things are no less real than the deliberate slaughter of one's fellows. They are no less real and they are more widely congenial to our powers.

VI

One more thing we should ask before we close. Will there be *motives* for extending the peace which now is confined within the nation's border? Will not the peoples of the world be content to have it rest there? Unless there are powerful incentives, the goal will never be reached; the powers in opposition—patriotism above the boiling point, the cult of sovereignty, the dogma that the ten commandments are for use only within the tribe,—these powerful opponents will prevail.

I believe there are powerful motives for advance, capable of becoming more powerful, year by year. They are motives, desires, long frustrated by the old chaos. Nations great and small are becoming aware that certain deep desires of theirs cannot be satisfied in a society disrupted, like a shattered earthen vessel. Let me speak of but three of these great national desires.

The desire for wealth is one of these, a desire not felt by millionaires alone or by men longing to be millionaires, but also by men and women busied with the plain human need of food, clothing, roof, health, play, and education. Men generally have not a tithe of what they should have of these. And in trying to fill the lack, nations stand in one another's way and trick one another. War is beginning to be recognized as one of the chief causes for failure here. Nor is the failure seen to come only from a nation's own wars, but from other nations' wars, from wars anywhere. And the frustration comes not alone in wartime, but in peacetime spent in expending wealth and effort in recovering from the last war and in preparing for the one to come. These preparations include all manner of things which impede the production of wealth and its flow into the most humane channels. Ten billion dollars a year now goes into world arming. A world that had become a community would not use in this way a hundredth of this mountain of wealth. And a world become a community could produce manifold more wealth than now.

The desire for wealth, powerful as never before in the world, will swerve, now one way and now another. But with intelligence and time and the heaping experience of war chaos, it will steadily point toward a world under communal law.

The desire for justice is another motive power. It is strong, but bewildered by the presence of danger at the gates. Let us imagine ourselves in terror of deadly combat with another, and then see how justly we shall think of him. Any concession which justice suggests that we make to him, must not be made; for it will increase his power. As things stand, we cannot be sure but that he already is too strong; we need every ounce of resource we have. France has said, this year, that she cannot help Germany in some of the economic things wanted by Germany, for France has no assurance but that this access to German strength would be turned against France herself. In thinking, as all the world does, of raw materials and markets and a fair avenue to these for all, shall we not be balked at every point by the prospect of war? Small nations cannot be expected to give from their small holdings. Will the greatest possessors willingly make the next-greatest possessors to be equal partners with themselves? Would these next-greatest possessors freely share their present great possessions with

Denmark, Czechoslovakia, and Switzerland? The next-to-the-greatest want all their strength and more, for their expected contest with the greatest. Not only the law, but Justice herself is silent in such a case.

Of justice this must be added. Even when in time of peace there is a will to be just, there can be little of justice where each claimant is his own judge and sheriff. Thousands of years of experience—we might call it psychological experiment—with armed bravoes and ordeal by fire, by throwing the plaintiff into the sacred river, by filling the defendant's mouth with dry rice, have convinced every now-civilized people that justice within its own land can come in no such way. Even sheer chance is juster than the desire for justice when this desire is dominated by self-interest. There must be the disinterested judge, the disinterested sheriff, set there by a will above the disputants. International justice can come only in this manner. It can come only through a community of nations ready to give office to judge and police, and to give support to them, in season and out.

The desire for justice, which now is found in many nations, is trampled down by the panic fear that others will be stronger than ourselves, indeed that they will be as strong as ourselves. It is deformed into a shrill demand for the nation's own rights, which is but half of justice, is injustice. Until there is a community of nations, the strong will get their due, together with much that is due their neighbors. The growing discontent with such unfair results is a motive for a world under law. Those who today are urging that justice come first, before we establish law and government, should remember that only by the methods of law and communal government can there be the just rearrangements they seek.

The desire for adequate national defense is the last of the three great motives for our purpose. It moves nations mightily and rightly. For with immense labor has the national life been attained; and this great achievement must be kept secure.

The strength of this desire is revealed not only by the wealth devoted to it,—ten billion dollars a year, as was stated,—but by the lives—forty-one million lives of soldiers and civilians, it has expertly been estimated—sacrificed in the World War. The desire to defend the national life is, one can hardly doubt, the most powerfully organized motive in the world today.

And yet its present action is almost futile. The case is as though the nations had used their best wits to make one another defenseless. The war machinery of the world, held in separate nations' hands, mounting in quantity and in deadliness, has increased the danger rather than diminished it. It is as though a mining camp, becoming at last impatient of its frequent murders, decided to end them. So each miner buys himself two automatic pistols instead of his one old shooting-iron. And then, finding that these have not accomplished the desired result,—for there are more killings than ever,—bethink them, each, to add to the two automatics a machine gun apiece and a capped stick of dynamite for use against the neighbor's house,—"insurance against trouble," they say, as they carry these goods home.

The nations will not continue along their present course forever. They will in time smile at the old patter,—that this mounting armament is insurance against war. For it neither prevents war, nor does it—like real insurance—pay the losses of war when war comes. Japan's armament does not prevent her wars with China; on the contrary, it is her means of waging them. And so with Italy. The most that can be said for the present method of national defense is that, to the few who can outstrip their neighbors in the race of armament, it gives promise of victory when the war comes. Against war itself, against recurring war, it can give but the slightest promise.

The real defense of nations can come only as it comes to individuals in a city, in a state. Here the body of citizens, with a common will to end lawlessness, organize themselves to defend any citizen, and to establish court, law, and police. Only when the society of nations, coming to a right spirit in its leading members, is ready to act in concert,—at first perhaps only in condemnation and indignation, and then in restriction of social, diplomatic, commercial, and financial intercourse, until finally, when all else has been tried, there is resort to action by police,—only by such concerted action, of which we are now in the earliest stages, can the nations be defended against the lawless. The desire for national defense, now unsatisfied, will urge nations to become a community.

These three desires—for wealth, for justice, and for defense—are available as motive power in our work. And with them are other motives expressed in the growing alarm lest our world's most precious cultural possessions be lost in utter disorder. The fear of what another world war would do to many nations, belligerents and neutrals both, is chilling the spirit of the bravest men. They do not attempt to face what would come to us and all others by a world war after the next, and by another, if strength still remains, after that. For there must be a stout will, an intelligent and concerted will, or this will be the sequence. But far on this side of such a doom, there would be chaos in the highest things of life. Our universities would be schools of fanatic prejudice, our morals the morals of the shell-shocked, our religion a cult of tribal and savage gods. War can do this to nations; we see it done in the mere preparation for war. Such damage to the spirit after further war would heed no national boundaries; it would spread, like pestilence, over continents and across seas.

Nations seeing the menace have begun to make common cause against it, taking hesitant steps. They have begun to see, our nation now with the rest, that none of them acting singly can avert the danger, that not all of them at once, but acting in disunion, can avert it. They are moving toward larger coöperation, toward a communal interest, and communal instruments to protect and advance that interest.

The great community is coming by no revolution; it is already here in large measure. Nature below man, nature in man, is not against its coming in larger measure. We have the powers needed to fill the measure full. Human nature and human culture, for all their stubborn resistance, offer us still greater powers of advance. The immense gains to be had call us farther along the way. What is afoot is led not by visionaries, but by statesmen of vision. The ideal of the society of nations become a commonwealth of nations, is attainable. It will, I feel confident, be attained. And Americans will be proud, I believe, to see their nation again among the disciplined resolute leaders in this great enterprise.